Joan's Journey – A Life well Lived

Joan Robson

Copyright © Joan Robson 2023

All rights reserved. This book should not be sold, reproduced, copied, loaned or hired out, or otherwise circulated without the writer's prior consent in any form of binding or cover other than that in which it is published.

ISBN: 9798385604364
Imprint: Independently published

Joan Robson

Reminiscences of Life from my childhood in Bewcastle, near the Scottish Border, through the war, through the decades and into the 21st century

Old Bewcastle (Artist Unknown)

Acknowledgements

I have to start by thanking my sister Margaret and brother-in-law Jackie Sisson and my niece Maria for encouraging me to write my story and Carole and Graham Somerville for helping me to persevere with it, compile it and finally to publish it.

On a personal note I am deeply indebted to the staff of Holmcare Ltd and the staff at Newcastleton Medical Practice for their care and support through Jim's illness and mine. Special thanks also go to my family and friends and neighbours who have always been there for us.

Joan Robson

A life well lived is a precious gift
Of home and strength and grace
From someone who has made our world
A brighter, better place
It is filled with moments, sweet and sad
With smiles and sometimes tears
With friendships formed and good times shared
And laughter through the years.
A life well lived is a legacy-
Of joy and pride and pleasure
A living, lasting memory
Our grateful hearts will treasure
(Author Unknown)

Early Days

I was born on the 8th May in 1934 at Brampton Cottage Hospital. It wasn't common in those days to be born in a hospital but my father had died two months before. There wasn't a road to Bushley Bank where my family lived so this seemed reasonable under the circumstances and of course my mother (mam) would still have been grieving the loss of her husband.

To give you an idea of the place my family was from, Bewcastle is a remote area near the Scottish border. It is an area steeped in history that has changed little over the centuries. A church, farm and castle occupy the site of a Roman Fort which was believed to have been built as an outlying defence of Hadrian's Wall. Bewcastle was also the core of reiving activity. Reivers were raiders (both English and Scottish), who raided along the Anglo-Scottish border from the late 13th century to the start of the 17th century. Many of the routes used by the lawless, feuding Border Reivers went through the parish.

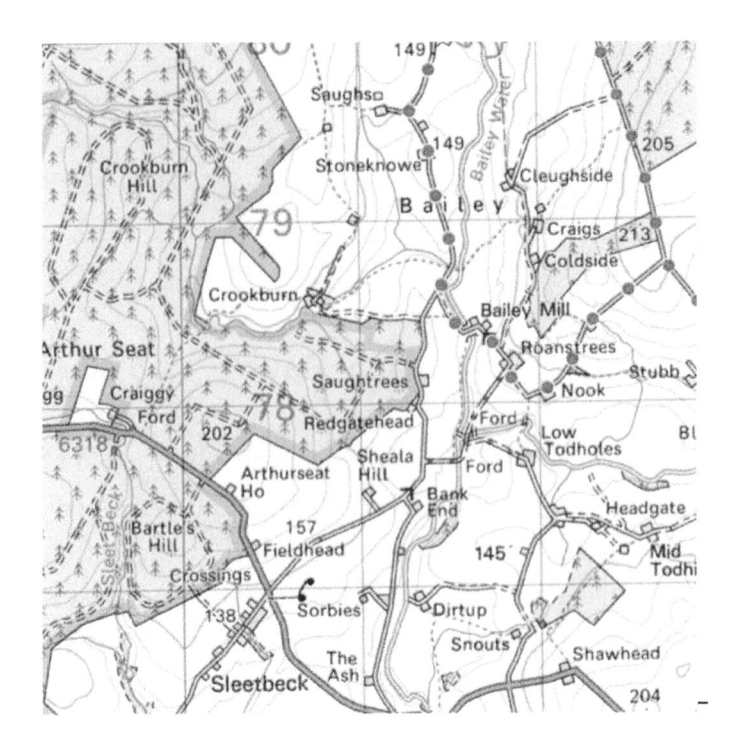

My mother was called Catherine (nee Little) though everyone knew her as Kate and my father was Jack Story. He was born in 1900. He lived with his parents Robert Story and Catherine (nee Ewart of Holmehead) at Crosshill. He had four sisters, Mary Jane, Kate, Grace and Maggie.

My father was a shepherd when he married my mother Catherine Little of Bushley Bank. Their family were: Harland, born 1928. John James, born 1931 who died of whooping cough at Redesmouth aged 11 months and myself, Margaret Joan (known to my family as Joanie) born 1934. After my parents' marriage, they lived for a short time at Gillsland then the family moved to Redesmouth Mill where my father worked for Lady Rowell at Redesmouth Hall. It was at Redesmouth that baby John died and soon afterwards disaster struck again for my father Jack suddenly became seriously ill with stomach cancer and not being able to work, moved to Routledge Burn and then to Bushley Bank to my Grandparents' where he was nursed through a very painful illness. He died just two months before I was born and he is buried amongst the Story graves in a corner of Bewcastle Churchyard.

My father was a cheery, honest man and was deeply mourned by all who knew him.

JOHN STORY (my father), Ina Moore, Mam (Kate nee Little), brother Harland.
Mary Jane Moore (John Story's sister) with son Alan Moore on her knee and daughter Catherine Moore, arms folded.

My mother lodged with the Shipley family in Brampton until she went into labour. My brother was six when I was born and my birth certificate records my father, John James Story, Farm Manager, deceased and my mother: Catherine Story nee Little. – The Storys are one of the oldest families in Bewcastle, going back to Reiving times. (Research I have done on our family history will be included at the back of this book). My mother's parents were Walter Dodd Little and Margaret Jane Little (nee Newton of Greenhaugh). There were nine in the family: Bella, Eddie, Flo, Peg, Jess, Kate, Wattie, John and Annie.

Bushley Bank taken in the thirties. John Little and Harland Story on the lawn.

After my father's death, mam, Harland and I continued to live with our Grandparents and for the first six years of my life, Bushley Bank was my home. I don't remember a great deal about it except that it was a small, ancient farmhouse. It never did have a road going to it and it is now a ruin.

Family life in those days was very different to the way it is now. There was no indoor plumbing, no phones, no car. There was no running water in my first home. We got our water from rain barrels and a well. Later, at Craigburn too, it was the same. Drinking water was carried from the well that was in a meadow downhill from the house. I had always seen open wells around but the one at Coldside was 'posh!' it was brick built with a felted wood and wooden floor. The water was always cold and fresh and had a very pleasant taste. Mother used to use the water from the rain barrel to wash our hair, "Because it was soft," she said! We were bathed once a week in a tin bath.

Grandmother used to have a pony and digby and a whip ... a two wheeled pony carriage ... at Bushley Bank. I don't remember the pony but yes, the digby and the whip. Horse drawn wagons and carts were the main form of transport in the early 1900s.

Mum (grandmother) – She loved gardening

We had an outside toilet with a wooden seat. At Cleughside, Bewcastle, they had a lovely stone-built building that housed the toilet. At Bushley Bank there was a stone staircase and at the bottom of the staircase was a sluice to empty the chamber pots. My grandmother never used it and it is the only one I have ever seen.

We had feather beds and all bedrooms then were with lino on the floor. Some of the downstairs rooms at Bushley Bank were flag floors and if you were lucky enough to have carpets, you would take them out for a spring clean. They were dragged across a clean piece of grass and then beaten with a carpet beater to shake all the dust and dirt out of them.

Bellows were used to get the fire going. No coal was bought. We used peat which was cast on the fell for the fire and I am told that one needed fifty cartloads of peat to last all year. Cooking was done on the fire, in the oven and on the big black fireplace. My grandmother (we called her Mum) would often make bread baked in the black oven. The warm smell of baking

Mum in Cleughside Yard

always making her home feel welcoming.

Scones were made on a griddle which hung from a swivel over the fire. Loaves were baked several times a week – there was no sliced bread.

We were always well fed. We ate a lot of bacon and game. There was plenty bacon from the pigs – usually two a year. Pig killing was a noisy affair. My brother Harland liked to have the bladder for a football.

Salting bacon was a big thing in those days. It would be placed on the stone tables in the pantry and covered completely with salt. It would lie in salt in this cool place for weeks then it was washed. The saltpetre (nitrate) used then is not allowed now as it is a dangerous substance, I believe. There was no refrigeration. The flagged floor and stone tables kept the milk, home-made butter etc. cool. Perishable foods were preserved by pickling, drying or salting.

Mam used to get work where-ever she could, often housekeeping. There were no Social Security handouts then. When she was at home she would take us to look for birds' nests. Visiting neighbours was a treat and we knew all the wild flowers as we walked across the fields. We often went to Collin Bank, High House, Woodhead and High Grains where mam's cousins lived.

My brother, Harland and I often walked to Christenbury Crags on the Bewcastle Fells and the first time I went there, there were cloudberries everywhere. I didn't realise at the time how lucky I was to see these. They were fully formed and edible. The fruit were peachy in colour like big raspberries and had a pleasant taste. I have seen the flowers many times since but not the berries. The locals called them noups. I have found out since then that cloudberries are one of the rarest and most sought-after fruit in the world! Queen Victoria is said to have liked them. I remember seeing goats, too, at Christenbury Crags but they aren't there now.

Christenbury Crags

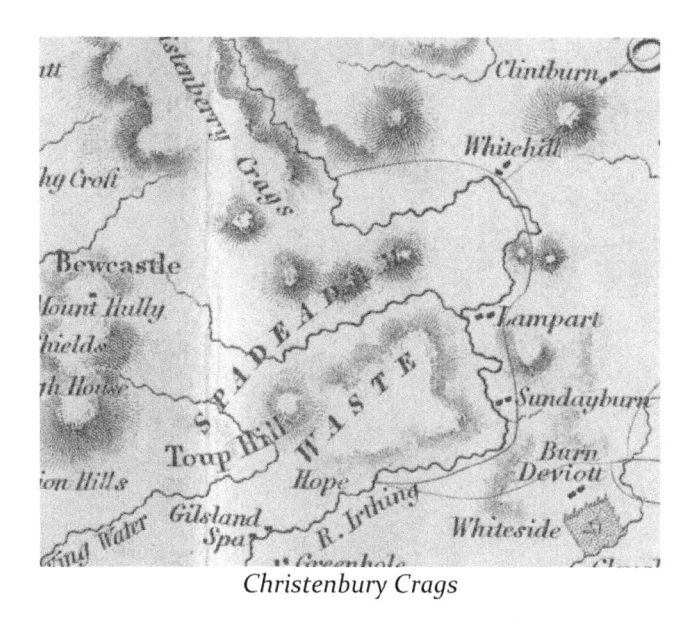

    Whatever the weather, we walked across the land to visit family and neighbours. I remember once walking to visit Auntie Bella and Uncle Willie Goodfellow at Blacklyne. On the way we called at Park Head, Sandcrook, Crosshill and Broadside When they saw us approaching, Uncle Willie came over the Blacklyne River and carried me across. I suppose this would give me a chance to rest my little legs for a while.

In early 1938 Uncle John married Jean Nicholson, a maid at the Bush. They were to take over the farm so Grandfather, Grandmother (we all called her Mum), Mam, Harland and I moved to Baileyhead. It was owned by Jack Kennedy of Cleughside who employed mam as housekeeper the year after his wife's death. As Essie was a young girl, Mam was a great asset to them. I spent many happy days there as a very small child.

(Bushley Bank, then and now, the farmhouse now sadly a ruin)

One of my earliest memories is when the Kennedys came to get my mother to go as a housekeeper for them. This was in 1939 when we lived in Baileyhead for a time.

Life at Baileyhead was great. I was five years old then and I remember a lot of the things that happened there. One Sunday in September 1939 uncle Harry, Auntie Jess and cousin Evelyn came to visit. We went in for tea and Mum said in a very serious voice that the Second World War had been announced. Of course, she would have vivid memories of the First World War which had ended in 1918. As the war continued, John Forrester of Bailey Mill was killed. At that time, Mum sent me down to Bailey Mill where the Forrester family lived, to get her pension. When I returned, she asked me what Jeannie, John's mother was doing and I replied, "She is singing hymns."

In the census of 1939, Harland (aged 11) was staying with grandfather, Walter Dodd Little (then 71 yrs, a retired farmer) and grandmother Margaret J Little (then 66 years) at High Bailey Head.

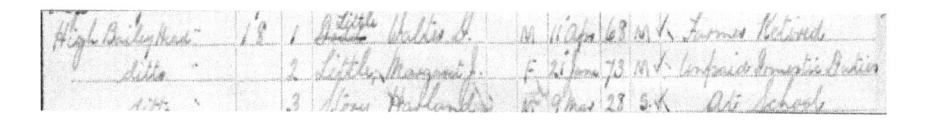

Mum was a great manager in the house. Grandfather was a good shot and we often had rabbit, hare, venison and game birds for meals. Potatoes, cabbage, carrots, lettuce, shallots, rhubarb, gooseberries and blackcurrants were grown in the garden.

In the summer we picked blueberries, cranberries, rasps and brambles which made delicious jams and puddings. Clouty dumplings and bread puddings were great favourites; cheap and filling.

One autumn we picked thistledown to fill cushions. It was a prickly job for little fingers!

The weather in summer was usually warm and we could play outdoors all day. We had no toys but I was always happy and rarely bored.

Mam went across the fields every morning to work at Cleughside. In the harsh winter of 1939/40 she opened the door at Baileyhead to be met with a huge snowdrift. She hastily shut the front door and went out the back door then trudged through the snow to Cleughside. That same hard winter, grandfather walked the frozen Bailey water to a sale at Low Sowerbies.

Joan at Cleughside. Winter of 39/40

One day Mum went to a Garden Party at Netherby. I was left with Grandfather. Well, I got bored, so walked across the fields to Cleughside. I remember walking into the house and they were all seated at the dining table having afternoon tea. "Where have you come from?" they shouted. Mam quickly took me back to Baileyhead to find Grandfather looking in the Bailey Water and Sykes, to see if I had drowned!

When Mum came home, she asked Grandfather if "the lassie had been good?" I don't know what he said as I ran down the pantry steps and hid under a stone table.

During WWII many concerts and other events were arranged to raise money for a Welcome Home Fund. To be payable to the local troops returning from war.

About that time I remember selling one shilling tickets for a soirée in the Knowe Church. I was given a ticket and went with mam. The entertainment was from Newcastleton and was enjoyed by all. There was little enjoyment during WW II.

We looked forward to Christmas every year. In our stocking would be an orange, nuts and chocolate coins wrapped in silver paper and not much else. I did have a teddy bear and a little red tin tricycle. Maybe they came from Lady Rowell who sent us a parcel for several Christmases after my father died.

Coldside

After a short stay at Baileyhead we moved to Coldside. Our goods and chattels were taken to Coldside and Willie and Bessie Armstrong's goods were taken to Baileyhead where they lived for several years before moving to 7 North Hermitage Street, Newcastleton.

Coldside was a fairly new house when we moved in, having been built by masons and joiners from Newcastleton. A man I knew in Newcastleton told me that as a boy he had helped on the building. He remembered getting water from the well and the wooden panelling on all the ceilings and walls in the house. There were three bedrooms, a parlour, living room, scullery and pantry. Up a ladder from the scullery was another bedroom. The steading consisted of a stone barn, byre, calf sheds, pigsty and general purpose buildings.

At Coldside when we went there, there was a midden. I remember seeing as a child what looked to me like a heap of muck. It was square and I asked grandfather why it was there. He said that the incoming tenant had to pay for it as it was used for fertiliser.

In those days too there was the cutting of rushes for thatching the stacks. Grandfather used to do that with a scythe.

While we were living at Coldside, Mam came home from Cleughside one day and said she was getting married to Jim Beaty of Saughtrees. Jim had been a good friend and neighbour to my father in their younger days.

Jim Beaty

With many foodstuffs in short supply, there was little to spare for festive occasions which meant the wedding took place quietly in the autumn of 1941 with only a few guests. I remember the wedding day. There was rationing. Not enough for a feast. Just an afternoon tea.

Shortly after the wedding, Jim, mam and I moved to a newly built forestry house at Graham's onset. Harland stayed on at Coldside. We were all happy there and Mam always called the house 'Happy Land'. Bewcastle, she always called her 'Glory Country!'

My half-sister Jane Forrester Beaty was born there. I remember the night of her birth very vividly. Our next door neighbour Phillis Castigan (nee Waugh) carried me in my nightclothes to her house. It was further to walk to school. On my way home I would call to see Mum and to ask if she had any little jobs needing doing. One was crawling under the beds to clean the dust off the linoleum. Each week I took Essie's homemade butter to some of the neighbours. I can't remember all the houses I called at but I do remember

(Margaret, Jane & Isabel)

calling at the Nook, the home of Lea and Henry, Robert and John. They had a maid who slept in the cribby under the stairs. It had a window. Most of them didn't. At each house, I received a big brown penny. When I had a few I bought National Savings stamps at school on a Monday.

I don't remember much more of our short stay at Happy Land but one very sad occasion was an accident at the Saughs. Fred Waugh from Lordstown was feeding the thresher when he fell in and was badly injured. He was taken into the house and laid in front of the fire but could not be moved. On his funeral day they closed all the curtains in the house. It was done as a mark of respect. Also people were bidden to funerals. A friend of the deceased did that.

We lived for a while at the new houses at Graham's Onset, my mother's Happy Land, then to Roansgreen but we had to leave there when the Forestry Commission planted Rispy Sike and Graham's Onset Hill, from Bailey Head to Coldside.

Joan Robson

Greenhaugh – Home of Mum Newton –
Newtons of Greenhaugh, North Tyne Family

Now this didn't happen in my lifetime but my grandmother, when she was expecting her second child, walked, heavily pregnant, with her two-year-old toddler, to her mum's at Greenhaugh to have her baby and then went home. This was the norm then and I have spoken to many people who have heard similar stories shared in their families. My grandmother would have no doubt rested in Shepherd's houses along the way, perhaps even staying overnight in some. I looked at a map and this would have been a 15 mile walk during the last stages of her pregnancy.

This was in the late 1800s when women from working class families gave birth at home under the care of older relatives. There was no pain relief then and doctors were only called out if there was an emergency.

Another time she told me about her brother-in-law who took his deceased mother and coffin by horse and cart over the fells from Bewcastle for burial in Falstone Churchyard.

Home entertainment in my childhood consisted of imaginary games like 'houses,' card games, radio, listening to music and reading. For music, we had a wind-up gramophone with a heavy pick-up arm and huge needle that played 78rpm 'shellac' records. Very primitive. At school we learned to dance with a gramophone.

If poorly Lucozade was always the remedy. We were given Syrup of Figs and Castor Oil, too, for constipation. Castor oil was a normal thing to have in the house then as a home remedy. If you had boils (say, on your knees) which was common at that time due to lack of nutrition with rationing, bread poultices or Kaolin poultices were used. (Kaolin poultices alleviated pain, reduced inflammation and cured abscesses). It was grey stuff heated in a tin and applied as hot as possible every time I had boils on my knees.

Boys, back then, seem to have had a lot of boils on their necks. – All down to diet; although we were well fed we will not have been getting essential vitamins and minerals.

You never locked the door in those days and when a friend of ours whose family had been in their farm for several generations sold up, they couldn't find the door key!

Merchants from the shops in Newcastleton: Fosters, Ewarts and the Davidson family where Cost Cutters is now used to travel around the farms four times a year selling household items, linens etc. Tramps used to call at farms and properties to sharpen knives. In our disposable 21st century society, blunt knives and scissors can be thrown away and another pair bought very easily but in the 1940s it wasn't uncommon to have mobile knife-sharpening services to call. They would carry a small grinder with them as they travelled from door-to-door. We also had a small stone grinding wheel for sharpening knives. Farm machines were always oiled before they were put away for the winter.

    We wore clogs all the time and each had one pair of sandals or shoes. Clogs were made by Willie Crozier in Newcastleton. Girls wore a liberty bodice or combinations – a vest and knickers combined with buttons across the bottom for when you went to the toilet. They were very warm. Hessian meal bags were used to make rough pinafores. I remember my grandmother scrubbing steps wearing one. She called it a scoogy apron.

Uncle William Goodfellow and Joan

The Home Guard – The Home Guard (the real Dad's Army) was established in 1940 as Britain's last line of defence against German Invasion. Many of the men who joined the Home Guards were those who weren't able to join the regular army because their jobs were necessary to keep the country running. They included farmers, teachers, vets and bakers. At night they would patrol fields where enemy gliders or paratroops might land or be in readiness to capture German airmen whose planes had been shot down over Britain.

This is Uncle William Goodfellow (in the photo), in his Home Guard uniform, with me at a very young age. He married Aunt Bella, mother's sister (Bella Mary Little) in 1919 and they lived at Blacklyne. He was a sheep farmer and I spent a lot of time there in my childhood, way out in the forest.

Pill boxes (squat little concrete buildings), too, were erected during the war and these were dotted around the land, their purpose to protect gunners while offering them a good field of fire.

Mum (Meg Newton)

Mam ('Kate' – Catherine Beaty)

After clipping time one of the ladies of the house would get a length of tweed to make into a costume. Tweed suits were both stylish and practical and were worn for formal and casual events. Tweed was popular among the countryside's hunters and fishermen as the fabric was both durable and water-resistant and perfect for outdoor activities. Men, in the early 1900s wore short hair and workers as well as gentry also wore suits but these would be of a cheaper, coarser material and had to be hard-wearing due to their jobs.

They wore caps and sturdy boots. Tweed suit lengths were made by Davidson from Newcastleton, tailors, or by Dan Beattie.

My grandfather used to wear a Shepherd's Plaid during the winter and lambing time. It was wrapped around his shoulders and he could carry poorly lambs inside it. He also had a lambing bag made of hesian to carry bottles of milk, lambing equipment etc. that were needed at lambing time.

There were no rubber hot water bottles when I was a child. We had a big stoneware hot water bottle called a pig that was filled with boiling water through the neck and the top screwed on and put between bedsheets to warm the bed. In the winter it wasn't unusual to wake up to see ice on the inside of the bedroom windows from frozen condensation!

All courses of a meal were eaten on the same plate ... first course, next course and so on, all on same plate; it saved on the washing I would guess.

When I was six years old, I started Bailey School a two mile walk away. (Bailey Board school was opened on the 1st April, 1878).

Auntie Peg and friend. Mum and Grandfather (Walter). Uncle Tommy Jobling. Mam (Kate). Essie Kennedy. Girls at front: Cousin Margaret Jobling, myself and Evelyn Binston.

Life was now very different. War was raging and there was rationing of nearly every commodity – food, clothing, furniture and petrol. This was real hardship although we had some foodstuffs from the farm. Every member of the public was issued with a ration book. These had coupons that shopkeepers could sign or cut out when people bought food and other items.

At school, Lill Ewart taught the juniors and John Lowes the seniors. Harland was in his class. Typical lessons included the three Rs – Reading, Writing and Arithmetic. In addition to these, we were taught geography, history, singing and sewing. The day would usually begin with prayers and religious instruction. During the war years every adult and child was issued with a gas mask. These had to be carried at all times.

Children were trained on how to use them and schools carried out regular gas mask drills. Because of the war in Europe there were evacuees sent to the country away from fear of bombing in the big cities. Larger farmhouses with more rooms would take in whole families. The smaller houses would take in brothers and sisters. The Whitaker boys came to Saughtrees and I often went to play with them - Hunt the thimble, I spy, Ludo, Snakes and Ladders. It was all simple fun. The Whitakers kept in touch with the Beaty family for many years. However, some evacuees did not stay long, others got jobs and some married local girls.

Rationing and shortages in most things affected everyone but Mum was very thrifty and could make do and mend.

At this time, the war in Europe was often mentioned. One morning Grandfather, known to us as father, asked me if I had heard planes during the night. I had and he said they were German bombers on their way to bomb Glasgow.

He spent a lot of time with me. He was a good knitter of socks and taught me to knit- plain knitting. He sometimes sat by the big black fireplace and whittled wood into potato mashers and rolling pins probably for wedding presents. I used to go to the mossy fields or the 'Hill' as it was called, with him, where he dug enough peat to last a year. He was good with the scythe. I had seen him sharpening it and then feeling if it was sharp with the tip of his fingers. I copied him and cut a finger – I had a scar for ages!

(G) Father always had plenty to do and I learned a lot from him. After lambing time, the peats were to cut. They were needed for the only heating and cooking facilities in the house (the big black range). In this hard time of rationing, coal was in short supply. (G) Father and Uncle Walter were good casters of peat. Planting of potatoes in lazy beds was another springtime job. (An ancient way of growing potatoes. With this method, large crops of potatoes could be grown in small spaces usually marginal or unprepared ground with very little time and effort. Evidence of this can be seen in many parts of this area). I remember him digging lazy beds to plant potatoes behind the Steading. I don't know if the crop was good. I have since seen the remains of lazy beds in Liddesdale. They can be seen where there was habitation years ago.

Clipping Time

Clipping the sheep was next when neighbours helped each other. Despite the remoteness of the area, the community all came together for the annual sheep clipping. Before the invention of electric sheers, sheep clipping was a communal affair and it was exhausting work. The sheep were brought down from the fells, sheared and marked. Harland and I used to roll up the fleeces and put them in a huge sack which was strung up from the beams in the barn. These were collected and taken to Hawick. Wool prices were quite good then. The dirty wool or clarts was not wasted. A general dealer from Brampton called Dick used to come with a horse and flat cart to collect them. I don't expect they were worth much. One time Dick asked mum if she had any gold sovereigns which he bought from her. They would not be worth what they are now! I also liked to help by putting the marks on the newly clipped sheep.

Hay Time

Next was hay time. There was a horse mowing machine, a raker, and a wooden sweep. Hand rakes and forks. There was also a cart and hay bogey. The grass in the meadows was cut with a horse drawn mowing machine, left to dry, then raked into rows with a horse drawn raker then swept into heaps with a wooden sweep and formed into pikes and tied with ropes made of grass. Harland and I used to rake up the loose bits of hay. I liked to ride on the bogey when empty and behind the pike when it was laden. The pikes were pulled in on the hay bogey and led in to the stone barn.

Haystacks were a common sight in many fields in those days. Hay would be kept dry for winter feeding under a thatched covering.

When mam, grandfather, mum and Uncle Walt were busy, Harland and I had a lovely outdoors life. We wandered in the fields looking for birds' nests and one time heard a corncrake in the Saughs meadow. We went through the fields past the house where there were Victoria plum trees, the same as those behind the steading at Coldside and through more fields to Holehead, a derelict house and previously a penny school (a plaque in the garden wall noting: School 1827). Inside was a barn owl's nest. We climbed on something to see several white eggs. When we returned home grandfather asked where we had been. When we told him, he told us not to go back because the mother owl would pick our eyes out. I suppose protecting what was to become an endangered species.

A Sad Day

Grandfather died one afternoon. Harland and I were taken away, I don't remember where, until things were completed that children should not see. I don't think he could have been ill for long but I do remember seeing Dr Evans from Newcastleton going into the house. He wore a brown trilby hat and came in a car – a rare sight. There were few cars in Bewcastle except the Kennedys at Bewcastle had one. A short time later (G) father passed away.

I don't remember the funeral. I may have been at school. Mum (grandmother) was very upset but she had good moral support from Mam who came home from Cleughside every night. She would have been a great comfort to Mum. Essie Kennedy was 15 at the time and she told me a lot of things mam had taught her. She said she appreciated how mam never told her to do a job but asked her if 'she would like to?'

I missed my grandfather a lot but being at school helped and when I had time to myself, I wandered in the fields looking for birds' nests and I knew where to find wild berries, fruit and nuts. I never touched the nests, but it was fun to find one that I had never seen before. The cuckoo sang all summer and once I found a young cuckoo in a skylark's nest – it was far too big for the nest! I also heard a corn crake in a neighbour's field. It would have landed there for a rest before moving on up north as that's what they did apparently. When I was casting peat, I used to hear golden plovers and curlews on a regular basis. Lots of pewits in the meadows too but there aren't so many now.

In the hay meadows in the summer there were many wildflowers. The outdoors was a great place for country children.

If it was a rainy day, I would go to Cleughside and play with Dodge's lead toy farm animals. Dodge was grown up but he still treasured his animals because they were the last present his mother had bought him before she died.

If I was around at milking time I liked to turn the separator to separate milk to get the cream for butter making. When Mam and Essie (Kennedy) were making butter, I liked to turn the handle on the churn. The skimmed milk was used in the baking of scones. If I was there at suppertime, Essie often made chips in mutton fat. I never forgot the delicious taste.

Granny Little, Kate and Harland

To get back to Mum (grandmother) known as the 'Duchess,' locally, Mum, too, was a great influence on Harland and me. She was very religious and taught us many things – The Lord's Prayer, the ten commandments and many quotes from the Bible. We had to say our prayers at bedtime: *'When I lay me down to sleep, I pray the lord my soul to keep, God bless Mum, Mam, Grandfather and Harland.'* I kept up saying this prayer for many, many years. She never worked on Sundays. I often think of the things she told me.

Although she suffered from 'the pains' (rheumatism) Mum made her own embrocation which she rubbed on the offending limbs for some relief. I remember her sitting shaking a little bottle containing a yellow liquid. I don't know what was in it but it smelled quite nice. The pain never stopped her from always doing something. She would do the washing with a possing- stick (used to submerge and pound laundry) in a dolly tub – hard work! The ironing was done with a flat iron heated on the peat fire.

She knitted socks and a rag rug was made every year. She taught me rug making which I was very grateful for in later years, when I was making rag rugs for Hermitage Rugs. She also made patch work cushions and one time she had a quilt in the rug frames. She loved gardening.

Every summer her sister came to stay and the two of them sat on the bench at the side of the house busy with embroidery and seeing what was happening in the Bailey. There was a lovely extensive view.

Mum baked scones and teacakes. The bread dough was set on the fender to rise. She made lots of jam because we ate jam pieces – slices of loaf with jam. I think we had jam sandwiches for our bait at school. Food rationing was hard for many people so we had to be frugal. Mum did have a store of tinned food under the stairs. Much would be probably past the sell by date but we never had food poisoning.

One day I had to take a message to the Ewarts' at Knowe Farm. Maggie Ewart made me a cup of coffee. I had never tasted coffee before and I watched closely as in the process, she reached down among the hot ashes in the big black fire grate and popped a cinder in the coffee. I remember she gave me some Christian Herald magazines to take home for mum.

Mum taught me a lot about thrift. We were encouraged to make do and mend such as knitting socks, darning socks and jumpers, sewing on buttons and saving money. I used to deliver some of Essie's butter to neighbours' and received a big brown penny at each house. When I had six of these, I bought a National Savings Stamp. Mum's sister, Aunt Mary came to stay each summer and often gave me half a crown! Equivalent of five Stamps!

ROANS GREEN (once a customs house)

So many places of our childhood that we used to call 'home' now no longer exist and Roans Green is one of them. There are no photographs that we know of existing of the house. Mike Jackson kindly showed me the extensive and interesting research he has done on Roans Green. The house where we once lived and where my sisters, Margaret and Isabel were born, is said to have been built in 1822 as a 'newly-erected dwelling house.' Just prior to this, the Roansgreen Estate was formed after the enclosure of the Baileyhope Common in 1814 and comprised 44 acres.

John Forster, the owner, purchased another allotment on the opposite side of the road, comprising 27 acres which had been awarded to John Gelford of Blacking, Stapleton, as mortgage of Low Baileyhead (West). By at least 1827 the semi-detached Roansgreen house had been leased as a Customs & Excise Station and remained so until 1855 when the duties on spirits in both Scotland and England became the same. The house was abandoned about 1959-60 and later demolished by the Forestry Commission. There are no visible remains.

In 1920 Roansgreen was sold and the sale details offered, "All that Freehold farm known as Roansgreen consisting of a Dwellinghouse, Farm buildings and 72 acres or thereabouts of land. ... The farmhouse which is substantially built and in good repair contains: sitting room, kitchen, pantry, dairy and two bedrooms. There is a good kitchen garden and the usual outhouses and farm buildings."

Barn at Roansgreen taken by Peter McDermott, 2015 Creative Commons Licence

When we moved into Roans Green in the early 1940s, life again was difficult with rationing and unavailable goods. I liked the outdoors, wandering about the countryside and playing in the big wood near Roansgreen. Our neighbour's children and I would collect old broken crockery, glass and tin and with a bit of imagination would have hours of fun playing 'houses.'

One time we decided we would like to smoke so I had to acquire the cigarettes. Millican's grocery van used to call on a Friday. I knew they sold cigarettes so I stole a packet of five woodbines. I was so scared afterwards thinking the police would come and put me in prison. I had been taught the ten commandments - Thou shalt not steal - so I was so ashamed and very sorry. And we didn't even enjoy the cigarettes! One learns from one's mistakes and needless to say I have never committed that crime again.

Jos Millican and Millican's Van

Our neighbour had a car and a school contract to take children as far as Saughs Gate, then the rest of the way, we had to walk. When not at School I used to help at home both indoors and outside. One time I took the big black cart horse to the smiddy at Oakshaw Ford to get shod. I was put on the horse's back and stayed there until my Uncle Bobby who was the blacksmith got me off the horse. I then went into Cissie's house until the horse was shod. Then I rode home again. No such thing as health and safety in those days.

My other sisters Margaret and Isabel were born at Roans Green so I helped with them. One day Margaret picked up a small serrated watch wheel, put it in her mouth and was choking. In panic we ran to a neighbour who had a forestry telephone and had to ring the Forrester at Kershopefoot who had a public phone to ring Doctor Stewart in Newcastleton. Jim (now Dad) was hitting hard on Margaret's back to try and dislodge the offending object when he shouted that she had turned blue. Then the next minute he shouted that it had come out! What a relief as we thought we had lost her. Another time Jane ran down the yard stopped and stood under the big black horse. Fortunately, the horse did not move until she was rescued.

I remember, too, at school, we used to all go out to gather rose hips. They were taken away to make rose hip syrup. Everyone was undernourished and rose hips is a natural source of vitamin C which was a particularly beneficial substitute for orange juice at the time. We knew all the places they grew and gathered loads.

When my sisters, Jane, Margaret and Isabel were small, their father had a cousin, Joe Moscrop who was quite a character. He used to bring small gifts (apples, oranges and nuts) at Christmas. He always brought a small calendar and an almanac. Grandmother used to swear by it. He would post gifts wrapped in brown paper to arrive on Christmas day.

Joe used to shepherd, at lambing time, for Beatrix Potter and was featured in a little book called *Beatrix Potter's Farming Friendship* which includes many letters written by Beatrix Potter to Joe. On January 30th, 1934 for instance she tells Joe, "*You will be as welcome as the flowers of spring!*" She speaks of a cold she has and then discusses her dogs and sheep before adding, "*I was thinking it would be worthwhile to buy 3 pedigree heifers at Road Head fair. ... you will, I hope, be at the Park, before the Road Head fair so will have opportunity to give us your views re Galloways.*"

Joe Moscrop had a little cottage in Bewcastle and he called it, 'the Mansion.' It was Redgatehead (not the one in Nicholforest) and I used to love to visit him; my sisters did too. He was a lovely old character. He always welcomed us and usually had something tasty to eat. While walking in the Lake District in later years, and seeing Herdwick sheep and sheep gatherings, I would often think of Joe and Beatrix.

Sometimes Aunty Bella would walk in from Blacklyne and call for me to go with her to Newcastleton. One time just before Christmas she bought me a net Christmas stocking from Lizzie Taylor's shop in Union Street. I had never seen anything like it so was absolutely thrilled. I only possessed a teddy and a rag doll which Mam had made from a flour bag. When the flour was all used the bags were washed and put out on the hedge hoping that the sun would bleach the writing on the said bag and then they were used to make garments, pillows etc. for cloth was rationed and very scarce.

Holidays were often spent with relatives. I remember Mam taking me to put me on the train at Newcastleton to go and stay with Aunty Jess and Uncle Harry at Reedsmouth. I had a list of stations I would pass. I had to change at Riccarton Junction and then went onwards down the North Tyne valley to be met safe and sound at Reedsmouth. What fun we had playing with a boat belonging to Lady Rowel. There were many frogs mating and we were kept amused by that. One day we went on the train to West Woodburn to visit Aunty Peg, Uncle Tommy and cousin Margaret. Cousins Evelyn, Margaret and myself were of similar age and great friends, a friendship that continued all our lives.

Apart from these holidays I was keen to learn and with the excellent teaching by John Lowes and Lil Ewart (later Mrs Lowes), I was taken to Carlisle Grammar School to sit the 11 plus exam. A short while later we got word I had passed. We expected that I would attend the White House Secondary school at Brampton which would mean I would need to find lodgings in Brampton. Mr. Bessie, director of Education for Cumbria contacted Mam and asked her to call at his office in Carlisle where he proposed that I go to Keswick school in the Lake District where I could board. This was agreed and Mam started to shop around for the school uniform. As we did not have many clothing coupons various kind people gave us some of their coupons to help us out.

The road past Roansgreen was topped with gravel and despite shortages the road was eventually tarmacked in 1945. My friends and I used to visit the steamroller driver who lived in a wooden caravan nearby. I think he liked our visits. One night I told him that I was going to a boarding school. 'No, never!' he said. 'You mean borstal!'

Most villages had a sports day in the summer. There was Penton sports and lots of fairs. Bewcastle used to have a fun day at the end of August. There was always a quoits competition there. That is long gone now. In my early teens, I cycled to Smithfield where there was a lady's bike race. I biked there, entered the race and won. My prize was one pound. Five a side football in summer was everywhere and there were regular matches in Bewcastle. Jim, my late husband, played in goal. Once there was something he disagreed with and he mentioned it to the linesman (who was my uncle) who hit him with a bag that had a bottle in it! Jim used to mention that many times!

The war still continued. Mam often asked Jack Foster, the postman, about all his sons away at war. He was very proud of them and like everyone in Britain, both young and old, they were doing what they could for the war effort.

In World War II it was quite normal to see soldiers passing by en-route on foot from Kershopefoot Camp to the Dog and Gun Pub. The Home guard which was composed of local men used to meet regularly in Bruntshiels, an empty house.

In spite of the war, life continued as best it could. A girl in Newcastleton was getting married. Someone perhaps one of the van men who called every week had told her father that we had a ham for sale. He came on his bike, put the ham in a sack on his back and biked off home. Mam said she never slept that night worried that the man would be stopped by the police and all would be charged with Black marketing. Of course, nothing happened and the ham would be enjoyed at the wedding reception!

Weddings were different in those days. The wedding cake was cut up and sent out in little boxes with nice cards on them to the people who didn't come to the wedding.

Nearly every farmer kept two pigs for slaughtering and for food especially during rationing. Dad was Chief Pig Killer in the district when several neighbours would help. Nothing was wasted. I used to stir the blood for black puddings and mince. Some meat was used for sausages and potted meat. Only the pig's ears and tails were not used. The trotters were eaten. I liked them and used to buy them in Newcastleton but I have not seen them for many years.

After school one night we were told that a plane had crashed on Kershopefoot hill. Off we went hoping to get a piece of the plane. Of course, we were not allowed near and came home empty handed. Many years later we learned that the young trainee pilot had died. Lots of planes from Cumbria air strips crashed in this area – young lads preparing to be bomber pilots and lost their lives.

At long last the war in Europe ended so on May 8th (my birthday) 1945, we had a day off school. In June the war in the Far East ended.

People were happier now that world news was better but shortages in almost everything were to continue for several years. I had never seen oranges or bananas for most of my life. We would even eat the pith from the skins. I still called on Mum often and tried to help her. I often went to Blacklyne to stay with Auntie Bella and Uncle Willie but one time Mum asked me to take a message. Remember few people had a telephone and the postman only walked from Stelshaw Lodge to Blacklyne on a Monday, Wednesday and Friday. On other days mail was left at Stelshaw Lodge. When I was setting out from Coldside Mum warned me about the cattle on Cleughside and Holmhead hills, Galloway suckler cows and a white bull which I kept well away from.

Bewcastle was famed and still is for its good cattle especially Galloways and Blue Greys.

A Major Arkwright I fondly remember, once enquired about the way to Roadhead Mart. He had travelled all the way from his farm near Edinburgh. Now petrol was still rationed at the time but farmers got a little extra. Someone must have told him there were good cattle sold in Roadhead. My step-father, Jim (called dad, then) accompanied him to Roadhead. Major Arkwright told dad how he had been a POW in Germany and had escaped. Later, he sent a book he had written, *"Return Journey from Oflag,"* which gives a detailed account of his wartime experience. He and two fellow officers successfully escaped from a German prisoner of war camp at Warburg in September 1942 and travelled back by night mostly with the help of the Resistance Movement. He ended up in Gibraltar (British territory) from where he got air-lifted home.

Keswick School

Greta Hall, Keswick

The day arrived when I was to go to Keswick School. Mam hired Rene Johnstone to take us to Keswick. On the way I marvelled at the height of the mountains as I had never been far from Bewcastle before. I was taken to the boarding house, Greta Hall (once the home of the poets Southey and Coleridge). It was a big house on a hill just on the outskirts of Keswick.

After a short time of my going away to school, Jim (now known as Dad) bought the 145-acre farm of Craigburn and we moved there in 1946.

At first, I was homesick and sometimes I cried but I soon made friends who are still in touch today. School was very different from the Bailey but I got used to it all and was top of my form that first year. Mam came for prize giving. Next year lessons were now quite familiar. Hence the list of subjects: English Language, English Literature, Latin, French, History, Geography, Chemistry, Physics, Biology, R.I. and Mathematics (geology, trigonometry etc.) We also had gym and games (hockey, netball and tennis). After five years I sat the Oxford School Certificate exam. I passed with distinction in French and Geography. Credits in English, History, Latin and General Science. Passes in English Literature and Maths.

Apart from lessons as above we had many other activities and outings. We visited the Border abbeys and tweed mills in Selkirk. The White Scar caves at Clapham, the bird sanctuary at Ravenglass, Wordsworth cottage at Grasmere and offices of the 'Keswick Reminder,' the local newspaper. Keswick Museum with its slate piano. Keswick laundry. Cumberland News office. Carr's biscuit factory and other places.

We had some interesting talks, one by Graham Sutton, the author of several books of Cumbrian interest.

Joan Robson

Margaret ready for school in Keswick

World war II ended in 1945 and a lady by the name of Odette told us about her time as a spy with the French Resistance. She was a French/British spy who worked as a Special Operations Executive in occupied France. After receiving basic training in England, she was taken by boat to France and for over a year worked as a radio operator using the codename "Lise." She was betrayed by a double agent in April 1943 and taken to Fresnes Prison in Paris where she was interrogated and tortured. After the war, despite her appalling treatment, she held no bitterness. She worked for various charities seeking to lessen the pain of war and was awarded the George Cross.

I recently saw a book advertised in the Daily Mail. Its title: *"Code Name: Lise: The True Story of Odette Sansom, WWII's Most Highly Decorated Spy."*

I don't know how she came to be in Keswick – maybe a holiday after her experiences in France. The lovely Lake District would have helped her get back to normal life. There were many other talks which I cannot remember.

We had Saturday morning School and prep each weeknight. We were well disciplined in every aspect. Our beds had to be made properly and the dormitory kept tidy. Punctual time keeping was of great importance.

In the hard winter of 1947, we spent a lot of fun time skating on lake Derwentwater. Every Saturday afternoon we were given our sweets coupons and a small amount of money from the ten shillings pocket money we were allowed for the term. After the purchase of sweets from Mrs Peel in Main Street we would set off on a walk. We had some odd names for some of them.

While out shopping we often saw the Borrowdale Hermit, Millican Dalton who lived in a cave on Castle Crag. He was very conspicuous in his peculiar dress and a big hat with pheasant feathers in the brim. He was usually smoking a cigarette. In the first year, Miss Barrow our English teacher often took us for walks, once to Scafell Pike, the beginning of my love of the mountains. Another I remember was to Watendlath which I loved and have visited many times since. One very interesting adventure was to see the sunrise on

Skiddaw. It was organised with military precision. - Happy days!

On Sundays we walked in crocodile style to Crosthwaite Church where the school had special pews. When the Second World War started, the Keswick Hotel and Millfield Hotel closed their doors as hotels and were used to house the staff and girls from Roedean School who had been evacuated from Brighton to be safely away from the bombing threat in southern England. The Hotels provided safe spaces for 350 girls between 11 and 16. Roedean school had the best pews in the church so when they left Keswick, we moved into them! We had to remember to have a penny for the church collection. Sometimes we only had a halfpenny. After church we had letter writing time when we had to write home.

While taking my exams Mum sadly had a stroke and passed away. I lost a great mentor.

I left school with many friends and a good education. I still keep in touch with those who are still around, sometimes for lunch in Newcastle and Leeds and at reunions in Kendal and Keswick.

After I left Keswick school I went camping with my closest school friends in a farmer's field on the shores of Lake Ullswater. We borrowed the camping gear from our scouting boy friends. The weather was decent. We could have a wash in the lake and have a small fire. One day we met a couple who took us to Windermere for a boat tour. They took photos of us. And posted them to us when they went home from their holiday. We learned that they were of Tate & Lyle Sugar company. Unfortunately I have mislaid the black and white photos. While at Keswick school I was fortunate to meet Jean Simmons and Trevor Howard and got their autographs. They were in the Lake District filming "The Clouded Yellow." Several of our friends were shown cycling past one of their sets.

CRAIGBURN

I was still at Keswick School, it was about 1946/47 when we flitted from Roansgreen to Craigburn in Nicholforest, Cumbria, but I must have been on holiday that day. I remember taking Jane, Margaret and Isabel across the Iron Gate Field and into the house where we had a boiled egg to eat for lunch. The girls were very young.

The place was run down especially outside. Willie Waugh of Lordstown, a very hard worker came to help and also Karl, a German prisoner of war. We all became fond of Karl.

One of the first big tasks was to repair the boundary fence. The fence next to the forest was good but the one next to Piperdean was very bad. Dad approached the neighbouring landowner who said he would provide the materials if dad would do the work. He and Willie Waugh and Karl renewed the fence which stood in good repair for 37 years.

A contractor came and cut down the hardwood trees that surrounded the house and steading. The money received from that paid for repairs to all the roofs.

Now new drains were needed in the Iron Gate Field so a team of German POWs came to do the work.

The only lighting we had was oil lamps and candles. When we went to Craigburn, we got Calor gas in the sitting room. – Electricity came to Nicholforest very late.

((Craigburn ... mam (Kate) and dad (Jim Beaty), Jane and possibly a friend))

This picture was given to Margaret by our father 50 years ago. It is a particular favourite of ours. It includes the winners of the Waterloo Cup for 28 years from 1861 to 1888 and is very rare.

At Craigburn we kept greyhounds. – Farms would do this to add to their income. - They were loaned out by their owners and we reared them. The owners would take them back for training and racing. There are two types of greyhound racing: track racing and coursing. In coursing the objective wasn't to catch or kill the game (usually a hare) but to match the athletic ability of the dogs against each other. They raced greyhounds at Waterloo. Those who had reared the race winners would get £100 prize money which was a lot of money in those days.

Greyhound Racing

Lots of people used to visit. They came uninvited which was the custom. I remember one Sunday, 36 sat down to tea – maybe three sittings. – We had a big dining table!

Roger Clark from Moss House would visit. He always smoked a cigarette in a holder which had been made from a hare's leg with a gold band round it. John Johnstone and Lottie Mitchel used to visit and play nap which lasted into the night. One time they stayed all night and had porridge for breakfast.

Most of the time I was away at School but when at home I would walk with the girls to see Mrs. Waugh at Troughead. Like me, when I was little, the girls liked playing houses and would walk across the fields to the 'tin bit' at Hollywell bridge. This was where locals dumped their rubbish. Every time they would carry home some broken crocks, even once an old cooker! During school holidays I helped Mam and looked after the girls. Sometimes if there was any spare sugar and syrup (rationing lasted a long time), I made toffee for them. What a treat! (They still talk about it to this day). Eventually they all started school and walked to Warwicksland School.

Warwicksland School

In the countryside many sales reps and travelling salesmen called at properties and farms. Their mode of travel changed over the years from walking or horse-and-cart, to railways and then motor cars. The changes would vary depending on the goods they sold and the territory they covered. One day, one of the reps came in the afternoon. Mam asked if he had seen three little girls coming home from School. 'No,' he replied which worried Mam because they should have been home by then. When they did return, Mam asked where had they been and the reply was that when they had heard a car they hid behind the hedge – what shy little girls.

In the house we had a POW named Karl who was with us for quite a while after World War II had ended. He was a nice chap who had been on a farm in Germany. When mam had some spare food, she would make up a parcel to send to his sisters in Germany where food was in short supply. Karl had a POW friend who worked at the Craigs. He had been a tailor and was quite gifted. I remember he made a pair of slippers from the threads of a hessian meal bag. The threads were plaited and sewn together. Some other POWs made wooden toys, dogs on wheels etc. Toys were in short supply in Britain at that time and these were in great demand. I also remember them making carved wooden picture frames.

I remember once at Craigburn waking up early one morning and on the bedroom window ledge outside were three small fledgling barn owls. The barn owl's nest was in the loft above the big archway and this was reached via the stable loft of the attached building. For many years they nested there but eventually disappeared. Only the one time did I see the young as they were learning to fly but it is a memory that has always stayed with me.

At Craigburn, outside the steading and behind the stone barn there was a circle on the ground (a horse gin - a wooden wheel device on a spindle that was pulled round by a horse) where a horse would plod round to drive a thresher or crusher.

Threshing was a big event every year when the farmers would get their crops in and threshing was a big community effort when everyone would pitch in. Very hard work.

There was a pond at Craigburn which was used for cattle to drink from but that isn't there anymore. Most farms had ponds and names for fields and there were gates everywhere. No cattle grids. From the public road to Cleughside there were six gates. -The postman and other motorists must have cursed them!

I remember dad taking Jane, Margaret and Isabel to the Knowe church for a Sunday service. They walked from Craigburn to Knowe church and back to Craigburn. The vicar was so impressed he informed the Cumberland newspapers and an article appeared in the news the next week!

The Craigburn Flitting

I want to include the poem, 'The Craigburn Flitting,' here, as it was a memorable and big event of the time and a great example of how the community would always pull together and support each other. This poem was written to commemorate the occasion which I think would have been the Dixons moving in. The number of helpers shows neighbourliness and kindness which was normal in rural areas. It is believed to have been written by M Nichol from Hollywell Cottage and B Waugh from Beyond-the-Moss.

The Craigburn Flitting

The Craigburn flitting, it did them a'ways Crown,
There was men, Horses and Carts, from all the Parish around
They flitted for days, when the rain didn't fall
For the Craigburn Flitting was the best o' them all.

There was young Willie Ward, Bob and Darcy Steel
And John from Catlowdy, ye all ken them well.
There was George Richardson and Joss did his turn
John Storey frae the Rigg, they were all at Craigburn.

There was Bob Rodden and Young Jimmy Hill
And there was Joe Wylie, we had his food skill,
Helped well wi' the Flitting, Bob Dixon and all
For the Craigburn Flitting was best o' them all.

There was Billie, frae Beyond-the-Moss and Jimmy frae Black House
And there was Jimmy Lawson, see Leigh and see Douse.
And John frae the Wood, John Kennedy and all
For the Craigburn Flitting was the best o' them all.

There was Allan Irving; he comes frae Trough Head
And Wattie Nichol, he ran at his speed
To help wi' the cattle; Sid Hill and all
For the Craigburn Flitting was the best o' them all.

How we cannot forget Lizzie Hill
Wee Berte and Minny they did them well full
With beef and good cakes, Mrs Richardson helped an' all
For the Craigburn Flitting was best o' them all.

There was Jimmy and John and Willie, so kind
They treat the men all wi' whiskey and the women got wine
It made them all talkie, and some prone to fall
For the Craigburn Flitting was the best o' them all.
(Author unknown)

My sister Jane married John Armstrong Lawson (Jack) in Nicholforest in April 1962. Our mother Kate Little died at Craigburn in 1963. Craigburn became one of the most popular restaurants in the area, especially for Sunday Lunches. Jane's sweet trolley was the most talked about and people got seconds too, if they wanted! Jane sadly died in 1999 and Jane and Jack's son Geoffrey and Louise with their son Jonathon ran the 150 acre sheep farm and guesthouse for a time before selling Craigburn.

  I am equally as proud of my sister Margaret and her husband Jackie who offer a 5 star Gold Bed & Breakfast and self-catering apartments at Bessiestown, Nicholforest. Just as successful was my late sister Isabel with her self-catering cottages in North Lakeland.

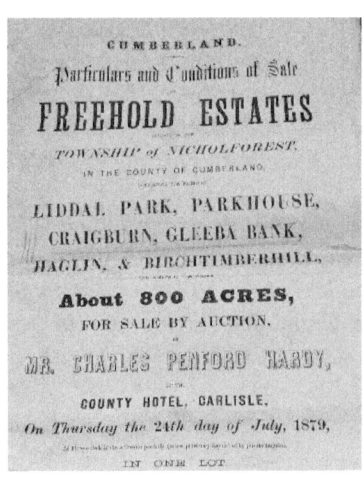

CUMBERLAND.

Particulars and Conditions of Sale

FREEHOLD ESTATES

TOWNSHIP of NICHOLFOREST,
IN THE COUNTY OF CUMBERLAND.

LIDDAL PARK, PARKHOUSE,
CRAIGBURN, GLEEBA BANK,
HAGLIN, & BIRCHTIMBERHILL,

About 800 ACRES,

FOR SALE BY AUCTION.

MR. CHARLES PENFORD HARDY,

COUNTY HOTEL, CARLISLE.

On Thursday the 24th day of July, 1879,

IN ONE LOT

(Sale of Craigburn in 1879 when it was part of the Netherby Estate)

On the Farm

Sweeping hay into heaps to make pikes.

(My granddaughter now lives with her husband in Tenerife and they do a lot of walking in the mountains. They have seen all sorts of old farming remains and methods similar to ours in past-times, on their walks). My father was a very good sheep man and this must be in the genes: my brother was a shepherd, my nephew, John, is a sheep farmer and his daughter is very interested in sheep!

When I left Keswick school I started work at the M.O.S at Sellafield. Part of my training was to go on a course in London, all paid for by M.O.S. A young man called Michael Levy, who I already knew as I had worked with him at Sellafield, met me and in our spare time showed me round London. We saw the show '*London Laughs*'. Jimmy Edwards was in it and we did so much more. By the time I returned home, the soles of my shoes were worn thin from walking to see as many London sights as time allowed.

SELLAFIELD

When I arrived in West Cumberland, I went to stay at Greengarth Hall, Holmrook, in a hostel for Sellafield workers. I had a room to myself and was quite comfortable. A bus took us into work.

There was a large number of young people living in Greengarth Hall and I made many friends, male and female. We climbed nearby mountains and walked around the local area of Holmrook, Rigg, Seascale, Gosforth, Beckermet, Eskdale and Wasdale to name a few. In my gang of friends was Phil. He had a motorbike so we could go further afield and often to his family in Preston and my family at Craigburn. We eventually got engaged which did not last long. Looking back it would not have worked.

At first, I worked in the chemical inspectorate at Sellafield, then, because I had passed the civil service clerical officer's exam I was transferred to the

Research and Development Department. As I was earning quite a good salary, I decided to save in order to buy a small motor bike – a BSA Bantam. I had seen one for sale at Rigg's Garage in Gosforth village. It had a price tag of £124. When I had saved £104, I borrowed £20 from brother Harland. Very soon I repaid him. I used it to travel from Greengarth to Sellafield and was able to go home sometimes at weekends.

I did not stay long at Sellafield as mam was needing help so I returned to Craigburn.

Joan Robson

Sellafield Days

Harland, my brother.

Harland always wanted to be a shepherd and it was while doing a lambing time in the Coquet valley that he met his wife Isabella H Reid (Isabel) of Haydon Bridge. They married in Haydon Bridge in Northumberland in 1954.

After their marriage they lived for a time at Elsden then they moved to Whitfield almost thirty years ago. Their family is: 1. Linda, born 1955 who married John Dickinson of Alston. 2 James Robert, born 1957 who married Pauline Scott of the Laws, Whitfield. She was a granddaughter of Sam and Frances Lee. And 3. John, born 1958.

Harland attended Park and Bailey Schools being taught by Ethel Armstrong and Mr Lazonby at Park and by Mr J. Lowes at Bailey. He was keen on hound-trailing and football but his greatest love was sheep. He also had a tremendous knowledge of moling. He and the two boys shepherded on the Whitfield Estate and were held in high esteem by Captain J. Blackett-Ord.

Brother Harland Story and his son James Story
Dry stone dyking is an ancient but dying skill that dates back hundreds of years. James retires in three years time and he has three years' of work booked!

CRAIGBURN AGAIN

It was nice to be back home again. I worked outside feeding calves, hens etc and anything else that needed attention. I helped in the house too. I had never had a local social life so I soon went to the local dances which were held in the school canteen, the Scugg hall (which was not very big and resembled an over-sized hen house!), Harelaw Hagg and Roadhead. It was at the Hagg where I met my Jim – an instant falling in love! Jim was known as Bizler in the village. A lot of people had nicknames in those days because so many had the same name. (Back in Reiving times there were a great many people of the same Christian name and each had a nickname to differentiate who was whom). Today this custom still exists. Not long ago, there were six Jim Robsons in the village ... Shiner, China, Lompy, Barrel, Bizler and Blondie!

We were married later that year (2nd September 1955) at Nicholforest Church and our reception was in the Liddesdale Hotel, Newcastleton. My cousin Evelyn, and sisters Jane, Margaret and Isabel were bridesmaids. Jim's cousin Sandy his best man. We flew from Kingstown, Carlisle to the Isle of Man for our honeymoon.

At first, we lived with Jim's parents at Valley View. In those days it was quite usual to do that, but we immediately started looking for a property to buy. We heard that 26 Langholm Street was empty. Someone told Jim who to contact. We went to see the owner who said he would like to sell it and to make an offer. Jim offered 50 pounds which he readily accepted. When the legal formalities were complete, we received the key and began the repair work. We had very little money, so I was fortunate to get a job in the Road Squad Forestry Office at Kershopefoot. After a year's work on the house, we moved in. Jim was still working on the Railway and one of the perks was cheap train tickets which enabled him to go the international football matches at Glasgow and London. He was a goalie in various local teams and latterly for Gretna.

26 LANGHOLM STREET

Shortly after moving into our new house, Anne was born at home. Jim had been at the bowling at Kershopefoot. When he came home, I was in labour and he had to run round for the nurse to come quickly! We bought a second-hand pram locally and managed with very few baby clothes and terry nappies which I kept nice and white on the clothes line. Having a baby to look after meant I no longer went to work and I spent a lot of time making the garden look nice. I remember one year I had a beautiful display of sweet peas but no success with them since. Sweet Williams were another success. I grew everything from seed. John Robson the shoemaker, not Jim's relation, who lived across the road from us was a good gardener and advisor. Jane was born two years later in the Haig Maternity Home in Hawick ... we got there just in time!

When we needed money, mostly Jim was lucky to get Sunday work relaying lines when the trains were not running. The pay was good and instead of receiving £6 a week we had about £12 so I now could save a little. I never got into debt. After having Sunday work, Jim started on the relief portering and was sent to most stations on the Waverley line. Again, better pay.

One day while working at Fauld Moor manning the gate on the road across the railway, a milkman from Longtown stopped and talked to him. When Jim told him we had no milkman or round in Newcastleton, he suggested we should think about starting one and to make some enquires, which we did. We called on all the houses in the village to see if most people would support us and if it would be viable. We decided that it would although some doubted our ability. I had saved £32 only so we asked the bank manager for a loan so we could buy a second-hand van.

I helped when I could, but we had two-year-old, Anne and newly born Jane to look after.

Jim repairing our house at Langholm Street

At first, we bought the milk already bottled from a small dairy in Longtown and as the venture was proving to be a success we expanded. We had a building behind our house, so Jim took the byre stalls out and did a lot of plastering to bring it up to standard. When it passed the planning authority, we were almost ready to start. We bought a bottling machine and bottle washer and built a cold room in the same building. We arranged with the Milk Marketing Board to buy the milk in ten-gallon churns from Harelaw Hole, Shelling Moss, Whitlawside, the Roan, Kingfield Guernsey Milk and local dairy farms. Profit was much improved and we built up a good business having bought a milk round covering Canonbie, Glinger, Penton and Kershopefoot.

We had some bad winters. Above is Winter of 1963, Jim's father on way to Hawick.

When we had the dairy, if Jim couldn't take the lorry in certain places because of the snow, he would put crates of milk on a sledge and walked to deliver them.

As well as the dairy business we rented some fields and kept sheep and cattle. I needed to learn to drive as we had bought a blue Ford 7 car. I went on the two o'clock train to Hawick, had a driving lesson and returned by train arriving home at five pm. Total cost was £10. In time I passed my test and was now much more able to help Jim. We decided to build an extension to the house. I drew the plans which were accepted by the authorities and Jim, who had experience from working with a builder when he left school, started to build a kitchen, bathroom and two bedrooms. When that project was finished, we bought three houses and equipped them as holiday homes and enjoyed good lets especially during the school holidays.

In all this busy life Mam was diagnosed with breast cancer. She had surgery and treatment but never fully recovered and five years later died at home. She had a great doctor and wonderful nurse who would cycle from Bewcastle to see to her. She was loved and nursed 24/7 by family, relatives and neighbours. Mam was a very popular person. During Mam's illness Jane married Jack Lawson. They went to work on a farm in Haltwhistle but returned to Craigburn when Mam died.

Next door to us in Langholm Street lived Davie and Jenny Holiday who kept Boxer dogs. I was afraid of them. A friend of Jenny, Ross, also had boxers. He was ex-army and had good army contacts so at Edinburgh Tattoo time he invited Jenny, Nell Adamson and me to go with him to the Tattoo! We had ringside seats acquired by Ross. The next year we went again and had seats in front of the Royal Box all courtesy of Ross and his army friends. On that occasion he took us for a meal in a restaurant owned by another friend. It's who you know!

We occasionally went out socialising in the British Legion at Kershopefoot Camp, the Dog and Gun and the Huntsman Inn, Penton (Annie Jane's).

Joan Robson

Joan (myself) with husband Jim and daughters Jane and Anne.

    I did get a holiday most years. I took Anne and Jane and sometimes their friends to Filey, Cowie, Oban and several other trips I cannot remember. I also went with sister Jane to Cornwall and Oban. In more recent years, Margaret and Jackie (who married shortly after Mam died) took me to Lympstone in Devon for their son John's passing out as a Commando in the Royal Marines – a great achievement. We then called on friends in Derby and Sheringham, Norfolk. We stayed there for several days, went on the Broads and visited several Country Houses. One day we took the train from Norwich to London and visited Buckingham Palace which was open to the public while the Royals were at Balmoral. We also visited Sandringham and Chatsworth House and Gardens.

    In most years I took a foreign holiday – more about that later.

In the fifties and sixties, I attended various evening classes – dress making, wood work – when I made a book case, kitchen shelves and two fruit bowls on the lathe. For several years I went to stick making and made several walking sticks. I gave many away but still have some to this day, one of which I got 1st prize for at the Holm Show. The late Leonard Parkins and Drew Oliver were excellent teachers of the craft. As I write, Drew still has classes in the winter.

Just some of the Walking Sticks I have made over the years. Many I have given away.

In 1962 the Railway closed (Waverley Line). It took six years from the Beeching recommendations to the actual closure which was in January 1969. Huge towns like Hawick and Galashiels ended up further from the railway network than other towns of a similar size.

Hawick became very isolated after the closure of the Waverley Route. It was nearly 50 miles from the nearest train station. Protests against the closure provoked night-time blockades by the locals. My husband Jim was involved in the stopping of the midnight train which was on its journey to London. It was a big event at Newcastleton Station Gates but did not prevent the closure.

In 1972 we moved to Union Street. We also received some sad news that same year. A local policeman came to our door to tell us that Jim's niece Davine, aged 25, her husband Trevor aged 30 and their 5-year old son, Gordon had been killed in a head-on accident on the road near Warcop camp. That was devastating news for all the family.

In the early seventies we had a big wedding to arrange. Our Anne married Billy Armstrong in Liddesdale Parish Church followed by a reception at the Huntsman Inn, Penton then Village Hall in the evening. They started life in one of our holiday cottages in North Hermitage Street while Billy and his dad built them a bungalow in North Liddle Street.

Then, after seventeen years running the dairy business, I went to work at Kielder.

My daughters Jane and Anne had ponies and spent a lot of their time on the fells on their ponies, training them and cleaning their kit.

Joan Robson

KIELDER PROJECT (1975 – 1982)

My first job at the Kielder Dam Project was in 1976 with Kelvin Catering in the works canteen. An office job came up which I applied for and was accepted. This was very interesting work and involved many aspects of civil engineering. When work on the construction was completed in 1982, the Queen came to the official opening. After the Queen had left, the office manager and I arranged an office party. Jean Elliot, who had recently opened the Copshaw Kitchen, did the catering and the whole event was greatly enjoyed,

Travelling to Kielder was okay except when there were snowy winters – the roads in the North Tyne valley were rarely gritted or ploughed and made for some scary journeys. One hard winter the office heating froze and I had to wear a sheepskin coat and long boots in the office.

When I had completed my job and seen tremendous changes in the valley, I was transferred by the company to the recently started work on the Canonbie by-pass. There had been a huge landslip on the A7 north of Canonbie, necessitating a new road on higher ground. When the work was completed, I took up employment with Halliday's, Longtown – a dairy and farm supply business. Unfortunately, the firm had financial problems and was wound up in 1985 so I was paid off (which pleased me as I never felt completely in charge of the job – spare parts for milking parlours and bulk milk tanks etc were quite alien to me!)

After this I did some part time work helping my sister Margaret at Bessiestown, also Lady Emma (Cavendish,) Tennant, Phillis and Alison. I always liked poultry especially hens. Anne and Sandy took me to a poultry sale at Longtown where I was amazed to see all the different breeds. I then got some Silkies and for several years kept them in the garden until I was no longer able to look after them. I loved them all. I had various other rare breeds and had names for every hen.

My parents and grandparents taught me so much including the value of working hard. I have seen them tired, exhausted, in pain, in turmoil and yet they got on with life without a thought. – They kept on keeping on and that is real strength. Life wasn't easy for them, food and supplies were scarce, nothing was wasted and they 'made do' with very little. I learned skills that I have carried with me all my life and have been able to pass on to others. Through the decades as I grew up, I experienced changing and different kinds of challenges but thanks to my hard working family and the supportive environment and basic conditions of my childhood, my siblings and I have never been afraid of hard work. We have embraced it. Growing up through the war years has taught me resilience and an appreciation for the simple things in life.

Another interest that stemmed from my childhood days was that I would often go with Grandfather or Jim to the peat moss where-ever we lived. So, I decided it would be a novelty thing to try my hand at casting peats. As a property owner in Newcastleton, we had the right to cast peats on the Bedda Moss. I discussed it with the Landowner's factor and sourced the necessary spade and began to cast. It was hard work but pleasant in good weather. I did it for several years and benefitted from good peat fires in the winter. I still possess the peat spade!

Treasure in the Peat Bog!

While casting peats I remembered dad telling me about the Beaty family's find in their peat, right at Graham's Onset. My father was a teenager at the time and was digging for peat with his two younger sisters. It was in 1917. They unearthed a necklace of amber, jet and rock crystal and a brooch. It is very unusual to find a necklace intact as the string often breaks and beads get scattered. Amber and jet are thought to have magical properties (as they are electrostatic and produce static electricity). Jet was also thought to have anaesthetising powers. The brooch was a silver medieval brooch with the words IESVS NAZAREN incised onto the outer surface. This is short for Jesus Nazarenus Rex Judaeorum (Jesus of Nazareth, King of the Jews). This was thought to protect the wearer from harm and the evil eye. They are on display in Tullie House Museum, Carlisle.

Peat bogs are said to harbour treasure troves of jewellery, swords and ancient items cast into the bog thousands of years ago (maybe as offerings to the gods). I did not find any treasure in my peat ... nor any man preserved in the bog!

Another pastime was bottle digging with my sister Margaret. We would go to an old, disused refuse tip and dig for 'treasure!' Usually, old bottles but one time Margaret dug up a beautiful Victorian scent bottle and Ladies Derby Day melanite entrance tickets which had been preserved in a now disintegrated silk hankie. What a find!

Over the years I shared many enjoyable trips with my sisters. For my 80th birthday Margaret and Jackie took me for a lovely few days to their friend's holiday cottage near Pickering. For several years they took me for a Christmas lunch to a lovely little café with friends, Walter and Hilda Shadforth in Rothbury.

When it was time to retire, at first it was very strange to be idle all day so I decided to look for work where I did not have to use my brain that much. I had had various cleaning jobs mostly during occasional mornings, allowing me time for my other pursuits.

As I had been taught the basic skills of rug making and became quite skilled, I was asked to make rugs for Hermitage Rugs and I made many over the years – this was a time when they were in high demand. I occasionally did demonstrations locally. However, the biggest was at the British Design Centre in Islington London.

A good friend of mine Jean Palmer went with me and we stayed in the Duke and Duchess of Devonshire's London house in Mayfair. Another interesting outing was to the Chelsea Craft Fair which was held in the town hall in the King's Road. Daughter Anne, Margaret Laing and I manned the Hermitage Rug stall and sold rugs to many interesting people; this time staying in Lady Glenconner's house in

Notting Hill. It was around this time I first met the Duke and Duchess of Devonshire.

I was also invited to Netherby Hall to watch a documentary film made about Lady Emma Tennant, *"Emma Tennant, Artist and Gardener."* Her daughter Stella was a worldwide model. Stella unfortunately died just at the beginning of the Covid pandemic. We had known her since she was a little girl; very sad news.

I have had many interesting adventures. My friend Barbara Smith organised many classes and outings including glass cutting, silk painting and mosaics to name just a few.

We had trips to Honister Slate mine where we spent most of the day actually in the mine and another time down an old iron mine at Frizington. When we came out, we were covered in red dust. Another was the Florence mine at Egremont which was still being worked mainly for the cosmetic industry. That was followed by a guided tour of Sellafield – a much different Sellafield to my time working there. Another interesting adventure was to a rag rug exhibition at Reeth. The exhibits were amazing. A similar exhibition had been in use the year before. It was a worldwide organisation.

We went to Elsmere Port Museum in Cheshire and Holy Island in Northumberland. We did the Farne Islands where we were bombarded by some of the birds. The Railway Museum at York and the Woolfest at Cockermouth. The Transport Museum and Kelvin

Hall Museum in Glasgow. The Museum of Scotland and the Botanical Gardens and Mary King's Close in Edinburgh.

I was lucky to go to football matches at Hampton Park, Old Wembley, Liverpool, Manchester City at Maine Road and several times, Carlisle and Gretna.

When I tell you about my holidays abroad I will refer to the Murray Blue Grey Cattle. There are blue grey cattle bred in Bewcastle today. I often wonder if the Murrays took a white bull and Galloway cow to New South Wales. Another breed I like to see is the Belted Galloway. When I was still driving I liked to drive up the Bailey to see them grazing in fields at Craigs farm. A lovely sight.

One outing I enjoyed was when I took my husband Jim to see the Chillingham white Cattle which are quite unique. Jim was not impressed as he thought they were ill-thriven but it's just the way they are.

One Sunday we went to Caldbeck for lunch then on to Bassenthwaite tiny church for a service in Cumbrian dialect. Melvin Bragg's daughter, Marie-Elsa, who is a vicar in London did the sermon and a lady played the harp. It was very well attended and made even more interesting as several of the congregation had attended Keswick school with Barbara and me.

Another good friend Stevie (Alice) and I did many interesting things including local walks and further afield, we went to Chester and walked the Walls, visited White Scar Caves at Ingleton, and we travelled on a special train to Oban. We visited many stately homes in the Scottish Borders. Essie had retired from Cleughside to Newcastleton and she also enjoyed all these trips. Appleby Horse Fair was another interesting one and outings to Chatsworth and Chester.

Stevie and I walked the Cedric Robinson lead trip from Arnside to Grange over Sands – a distance of ten miles. I did it again with Carlisle Ramblers. Stevie and I went to Liverpool for a sail on a ferry up the Manchester Ship Canal as far as Salford Quays in Manchester. It was mostly through an industrial area but very worthwhile.

Rodney Jeremiah had a pilot's licence and he took Jim and I on a flight up the valley and over the village several times. Another time he flew over part of the Lake District down to Morecambe Bay and back up the West Cumbrian coast. Another flight I enjoyed, this time by helicopter, was with the Time Team who came to Newcastleton to do a programme for TV about the Border Ballads.

Joan Robson

Joan Robson of the Hobbie Noble Team with Mick Aston

The Hobbie Nobles Team. Left to right: Barbara Smith, Joan Robson, Duncan Telford and Iver Gray.

I was asked to take part in the Ballads of Hobbie Noble who had been banished from his native Bewcastle to Scotland where he stayed at the Mains Farm up the Liddel valley. The story goes he thought he had escaped up the Kershope Burn still in Scotland then across the Border into Bewcastle where he was caught. He had been betrayed by Sim of the Mains. I was fortunate to go in the helicopter and comment on the route he would have taken. I knew the territory but not from the air.

Later I was filmed about the creation of Newcastleton for a Dales programme on TV and after th is, a local author and historian interviewed me for TV, on what I remembered of World War II. I was young during the war but did remember a variety of certain things. The interviewer thought I looked too young to remember!

LIDDESDALE HERITAGE ASSOCIATION

As well as evening classes in Crook Making and woodwork, there was Scottish country dancing and talks on local history. It was Dr Michael Robson who suggested we form a Heritage Society. A committee of twelve was formed and we had use of a hut at the village hall, then in a small shop in Douglas Square. When the local churches were linked to become Liddesdale Parish Church the Liddesdale Heritage society was offered the congregational church which we converted into a museum.

The logo represents a steel bonnet (as worn by Reivers) and a white orchid after those found on the Holm Hill. We restored the local Armstrong Memorial, a monument in Castleton Cemetery. – The Armstrongs were doctors of paediatric fame. George Armstrong was the founder of the world's first hospital for sick children.

Another restoration was that of the Oliver Mausoleum near Dinabyre Farm. We also assisted Fiona Armstrong in forming of the Reiver Trail.

The committee composed a list of local walks and I led walks around Newcastleton for members of the Elliot Clan Gathering and the Bewcastle Heritage Society.

Local walks included Riccarton, Davidson Monument, the Border line, Liddell Bank, Old Settlements – there are over 300 old settlements in Liddesdale and some you can still see where they have been and where they milked the sheep (now just mud and stone mounds). Behind them is where the lazy beds had been. Stevie and I walked all over Liddesdale and once when we were out walking, someone said to us, "Are you pair out again? You must know every blade of grass in Liddesdale!"

We recently welcomed to the Heritage Centre, Richard Henderson and his wife. Richard had attended the local school and Hawick High School and had been awarded the Nobel Peace Prize for Chemistry. – A great achievement! - A generous donation was received.

In 1993 we completed a tapestry depicting various stories from Newcastleton in the 200 years since the village was started. This was unveiled by the Duke of Buccleuch. We were given an Oliver Plough which was restored by Billy Lockerbie. Several members of our committee and myself were invited to Holyrood for the ceremony of the handing over of the keys. The Queen would usually have been in attendance but the Duke of Buccleuch represented her this time.

One time we organised a Burns Supper which was well attended and enjoyed. Another time we entertained Eric Robson when he launched his book the Border Line. Eric was born in Newcastleton and was a relative of my late husband.

Over the years we had visits and communications from many people from across the globe who were doing their family history. One of our projects was recording the inscriptions on local headstones. The list was compiled over two summers and was made into two volumes. Castleton and Saughtree and the other, Ettleton. These are available through the Scottish Genealogy Society. After completion of the above, my friend Stevie, Chester Forster and myself transcribed the inscriptions on Nicholforest tombstones.

I was also asked by the Nicholforest Parish Council to do an update on the conditions of Nicholforest Rights of Way. There are 37 Rights of Way in this parish and a friend and I spent the whole of one winter on this project.

Earlier, in 2001, the outbreak of foot and mouth disease caused a crisis in British farming and in tourism, both of which our community depended upon. Hundreds of farms throughout Cumbria and on the Border were struck with this horrific disease, generations of work was wiped out as millions of animals were slaughtered. It was a sad day when they came to take our sheep away. We had around 30 sheep at the time; they were pets almost. Jim had a Leicester Ram who used to climb up to Jim. Jim would offer him crusts of bread and he would take it off him. We used to have cattle as well. We rented fields off the Buccleuch Estate and bought some fields later on. Losing our sheep during the foot and mouth outbreak was more or less the end of Jim keeping sheep.

On my retirement amongst many other pursuits, as mentioned above, I did a lot of walking. During several summers I led walks on Monday evenings joined by locals and anyone wishing to take part. They were always well attended. The walks included Newcastleton, Langholm, Nicholforest, Bewcastle, Bonchester and Kielder.

One day Barbara rang and asked if I would take some of her friends to Christenbury Crags which I happily did. They were members of Carlisle and District Rambling Club and they invited me to join them the following week and we met at the Sands Centre car park in Carlisle at 9 am on the Sunday morning and drove to Wasdale Head and walked up to the foot of Scafell (not Scafell Pike). From there we scrambled up the West Wall, Lord's Rake and the West Wall Traverse. I enjoyed the adventure so much that I decided to join the Ramblers. I went with them for several years until I had to have surgery on my knees.

I have many happy memories of times in the Lake District, Yorkshire Dales and Scottish Borders to name but a few. Week long walking holidays at Malham, Whitby and Pitlochry were arranged on a yearly basis. Six of us spent a week on the Isle of Skye. – The Cullins really are mountains! One year we were taken by bus to Glenmore Lodge and walked the Lairig Ghru Walk from Glenmore to Linn of Dee near Balmoral

Castle. The following year we did it in the opposite direction. – 20 miles and recommended to be walked only in the summer months!

I walked from Bewcastle Church once to Newcastleton and raised a good sum of money which I gave to Bewcastle Church towards the cost of a new stained glass window. (I have an allegiance with Bewcastle Church as I have many relatives interred there). The weather was sunny and the birds were singing. I particularly remember the sky larks in full voice on Park Farm land, something I have not experienced in a long time.

Getting out and walking isn't just good for physical health, it is good for the soul. I've been lucky to live in beautiful places, surrounded by nature, all my life. We faced many hardships in my childhood, the 1940s being a decade of challenge and adversity for everyone who lived through it but there was always a sense of freedom when out in the countryside. I have always felt an emotional closeness with the natural world and through my life have enjoyed any chance to share this with others.

I served on Newcastleton Community Council for over 30 years. I was at the first meeting for the Campaign for Borders Rail which I strongly hope will be successful.

For many years I have enjoyed reading Chris Bonington's mountaineering books, *The Conquest of Everest*, etc. So I was delighted to be asked to the opening of New Walks Marked Paths in Netherby woods. Chris Bonington and his wife were guests of honour. I had a very pleasant day in their company.

While writing this I remembered a slide show I had seen given by Doug Scott. It was in Stapleton Hall and the funds raised were for a charity in Nepal.

When Jim and I had been married for fifty years, the family organised a get together lunch in the Grapes Hotel. Freda and Sandy Hardy and Evelyn and John Moore were included. Sandy had been Jim's best man and Evelyn my chief bridesmaid. Jane, Margaret and Isabel, the little bridesmaids. At our diamond wedding, Margaret and Jackie (it was their golden wedding anniversary) shared and organised a hog roast party at Bessiestown for nearly two hundred friends and family. It was a glorious day and everyone was able to enjoy the outdoors.

Covid-19

In March 2020 the World Health Organisation declared covid-19 a pandemic. On 18th March, Boris Johnson announced the indefinite closure of schools to curb the spread of the virus and on 23rd March he announced the UKs first national lockdown. We were only allowed to leave our homes for strictly limited reasons. Jim and I were interviewed and had our photo taken for a local Newspaper for a piece they were doing about managing during the lockdown.

Joan Robson

FORMER community councillor and keen walker Joan Robson of Newcastleton said she and her husband, Jim, were "bearing up".

Joan said: "We're staying at home, although I'm going out for little walks.

"I phone my order for groceries to the shops and pay by card and they deliver them.

"I use the Spar and Costcutter and I can get everything I need from them."

Joan says they have very good neighbours next door and they keep an eye out for the elderly couple.

She said: "We're managing fine and, apart from not being able to visit my sister in Penton once a week, life is not that much different.

"Jim is frail and his movement is very bad so he doesn't get out of the house. We don't have carers for him.

"Last year I had the house altered to make life easier and there is now a bathroom and bedroom downstairs.

"We're more fortunate than some. I've just been out today and we have these long-distance conversations with people dotted about at different points.

"We can do that because the weather is nice so we're not isolated really.

"There are also people coming round twice a day to check on everyone and there have been different things for people to do.

"In fact, the volunteers have done a very good job but I don't think life will ever be the same. There will be a lot of changes."

Jim and Joan Robson of Newcastleton are grateful to have such good neighbours

The Pandemic 2020

'Former community councillor and keen walker Joan Robson of Newcastleton said she and her husband, Jim, were "bearing up."

Joan said: "We're staying at home, although I'm going out for little walks. I phone my order for groceries to the shops and pay by card and they deliver them. We're managing fine and, apart from not being able to visit my sister in Penton once a week, life is not that much different. Jim is frail and his movement is very bad so he doesn't get out of the house. We don't have carers for him. Last year I had the house altered to make life easier and there is now a bathroom and *bedroom downstairs. We're more fortunate than some. I've just been out today and we have these long-distance conversations with people dotted about at different points. We can do that because the weather is nice so we're not isolated really. There are also people coming round twice a day to check on everyone and there have been different things for people to do. In fact, the volunteers have done a very good job but I don't think life will ever be the same again. There will be a lot of changes.'*

Jim and I received a congratulatory card from the Queen which I cherish to this day.

Unfortunately, Jim took ill with dementia and Parkinson's and eventually passed away on May 5th 2020 aged eighty-eight. As the Pandemic, Covid, was at its worst, we were only allowed to have ten mourners at Ettleton Cemetery and no contact with anyone and no funeral tea. Vicky Pounder conducted the funeral and made a lovely job in such difficult circumstances. Very many locals lined the street to pay their respects as the cortege passed en route to Ettleton.

Online there were so many condolences offered by members of the Copshaw Community Facebook Group. Jim was described as a 'colourful character, known to most of us as Bizler, a much beloved local man who had time for everybody he met,' and he would be missed by them all. Some shared their memories. Mark Palmer 'spent four years delivering "the milk" and it was always quite a hurl when Jim drove the lorry!' Jim took him to his first Celtic game v FC Rosenberg, 'played at Hampden Park in European Cup when I was eleven.'

Valerie Collins said he was a 'proper Copshaw character,' and Robert Robson said that 'when I worked with him on the milk round, he always stopped and spoke. A true gentleman.' Julie Hallam was 'so sorry to hear Jim had passed away. Bizler was such a character. He used to tell me some tales about the Wembley turf in my back garden at Langholm Street, also the spirit level he left buried in the wall over one of the doors in my house; and how much he paid for the house when they first bought it. He was a "belting chap", and would be sadly missed.'

Others shared happy memories of 'Bizler,' playing in goal for Hearts of Liddesdale back in the early 1960s and the stories he told about his Wembley trips. – Those who didn't know him would think they were made up ... but they were all true.

James McVittie (Bizler) Robson
A Copshaw Holm Man
1931-2020

Life was very different now but good neighbours, relatives and friends were a great comfort and support. What with the hardships of Covid lockdown and two huge floods where the river broke its banks (many homes flooded and residents had to leave their homes until they were again habitable), the authorities appointed several ladies to visit those who needed a bit of moral support and comfort. One of these ladies was Claire, later accompanied by Lindsay. I did appreciate their visits. I will never forget all the telephone calls from Margaret and Isabel and family friends – phone calls because no one was allowed to visit while lockdown continued.

Newcastleton, early 1900s

HOLIDAYS ABROAD –

I can only give a summary of my many holidays abroad or I would fill another book on these alone!

SWITZERLAND – Lugano on the Border with Italy. Beautiful scenery. At the same time we took a trip to Venice, Italy and St Mark's Square. The Doge's Palace in Venice, the Murlano Glass Works. A Gondola trip on a canal and the Rialto Bridge, Venice.

A trip to St. Moritz over steep passes and past fields of wild flowers. A boat trip on Lake Lugano – stunning scenery.

Joan Robson

TENERIFE – A leisure holiday at Puerto de la Cruz. Also several times at Los Gigantes. I went across to La Gomera, one of Spain's Canary Islands and toured the island. The natives in the remote parts communicate by whistling.

HOLLAND – A day trip to Keukenhof to see the tulips.

FRANCE – A day trip to Paris and saw most of the famous places.

ITALY – A school friend who lives in Rome took us to the main places. – Trevi fountain, Spanish Steps, Colosseum. Palatine Hill, Rome, the Vatican and the Sistine Chapel. – all in a week!

MADEIRA – Stayed in Funchal near the Harbour. Many cruise ships call there. Did tour around the island. Visited the Valley of the Nuns. One Sunday we listened to lovely singing by the nuns. It was Chestnut Festival time. There were many tasty goodies for sale, all containing chestnuts. Took the cable car from Funchal to the beautiful gardens. Watched sledging.

GAMBIA – Leisure holiday. Visited the village where Roots was filmed. Did a Safari. Lovely people. Also in

Gambia, a Sunshine Holiday. Toured around Gambia and visited a school. Crossed the Gambia River by ferry and toured the other part of Gambia near the border with Senegal.

TUNISIA – Sunshine Holiday.

USA – Florida: Disney World, the theme parks. Did all the rides. Water World, Universal Studios and shopping in Orlando.

Also in USA, San Francisco. Lombard Street and rode on the outside of a cable car. Golden Gate Bridge, Chinatown. Travelled to Yosemite National Park, Majave dessert. Death Valley, Bryce Canyon. Helicopter over Grand Canyon. Las Vegas, where we watched the gambling. Los Angeles, Hollywoodand up the Pacific Cast to San Francisco. The entire tour took in four states.

BRAZIL – Rio di Janeiro. Copacabana Beach. Maracana Football Stadium. A concert by actresses in exotic costumes – very good. Football games on the beaches. A tour through a rainforest and coffee growing region to Petropolis. A sail round some islands. Had lunch on one and I saw jackfruit for the first time. In Rio there are the very rich and the very poor. The poor live in favelas (huts made out of anything). We went to Sugarloaf Mountain by cable car (James Bond fame) and did the helicopter flight. And the Funicular railway to Christ the Redeemer statue.

IBIZA – Sunshine Holiday.

CORFU – Sunshine Holiday.

INDIA – Incredible India. Delhi. Very busy with all sorts of traffic with dogs, pigs, hens, goats and cows all roaming freely. Cows have pride of place. Visited many temples and historic buildings and an outdoor school on the bare ground. From Delhi we went to Jaipur and saw the Pink Palace, the Hawa Mahal (the Palace of the winds). From there to the Taj Mahal at midday and again next morning. Then back to New Delhi and Old Delhi. When we came home we held a slide show in the village hall and the money raised was sent to the tour guide (who was trying to promote the school we visited). The money enabled them to build a shack as during the monsoon the children could not attend school as they had no building to keep them safe. There are a lot of children in India who are keen to learn but not all get a chance to go to school.

SOUTH AFRICA – Table Mountain Cape Town by revolving cable car. Kirstenbosch Botanical Garden which was huge and amazing. Robben Island where Nelson Mandela was in prison. Saw the prison cells and limestone quarry where he had to work. Went to Simon's Town to see the penguins and down to the Cape where there are many beautiful wild shrubs and flowers. Went to a huge market in Green Park and the nearby re-developed water front in Capetown. From Capetown we did the Garden Route to Knysna then Franschhoek and the winelands. Returned to Capetown.

SPAIN – Murcia, Cartagena and stayed in Mazagon.

ZIMBABWE – Harare then to Victoria Falls and the Elephant Hills Hotel. Safari in Hwange National Park. Saw many wild animals. Went to a crocodile farm and to a snake pit containing 24 different snakes found in Zimbabwe. Flew by helicopter over the falls. Flwe back to Harare for the flight home.

ZAMBIA – Crossed the Zamezi River by the bridge which was made in Darlington and shipped out to Rhodesia as it was known then. Did a safari then was entertained in the garden of a British couple. Visited a native village with thatched huts.

Joan Robson

BOTSWANA – From Victoria Falls to the Borders of Botswana was not far. Joined a boat on the Chobe River. Many hippos and elephants close-up. A rich country compared with its neighbours. Then flew from Victoria Falls to Harare and to Heathrow.

SOUTH AFRICA (again). Flew to Johannesburg. Went to Pretoria museums etc then went across country to Kruger Park. Did several safaris and saw the big five and many more species. Moved to the south of the park and saw more. Early one morning we had a good view of a pride of lions having their breakfast of some poor wild beast.

After the stay in Kruger we went to Blyde Canyon and God's Window with a view as far as Zimbabwe. Then back to Johannesburg to fly to Capetown for a few days rest. We went to Kirstenbosch Gardens again. South Africa is nice but there are many townships – cardboard and tin shacks.

AUSTRALIA – My daughter Jane and I flew to Melbourne for my granddaughter's wedding. (See weddings). As well as the wedding, we saw much of the city by tram. St Kilda etc. We did the Great Ocean Road trip which was very scenic. Another was to Ballarat and to a theme park based on goldmining long ago (similar to Beamish). Another was by train to Bendigo, an old gold mining town. It was here we went down an old gold mine, alas no gold nuggets. Another outing by car to Echuca in New South Wales. We had a cruise by paddle steamer on the Murray River. Murray River was named by immigrants from Eskdalemuir! They were connected to the Murrays of Liddesdale, hence the name Murray River. I often wonder if they took with them a white shorthorn bull and Galloway cows, hence 'Murray Blue Cattle.'

DUBAI – This was a three-day stop over when we came back from Australia. We went into the desert and also did a trip up the Wady Dry Riverbeds. So, at some time there must have been rain in that part of the world!

FRANCE – Cannes, Grasse. Antibes and the beautiful yachts. Monaco.

ITALY – Naples. Etna. Capris. Sorrento. Palermo. Pompei and Herculanum.

RHODES – Sunshine holiday.

EGYPT – Cairo. Giza, the Sphinx, thePyramids. Aswan Dam, one of the world's largest embankment dams, Abu Simbel (the site of two temples built by the Egyptian King Ramses II. Sailed in a dhoni on the Nile. Tour of Luxor. Valley of the Kings. Cruise on the Nile from Luxor to Cairo.

And then back to England and KESWICK – I had a birthday treat, by my friend Doris, who took me to Keswick. We stayed there a few days and wandered the town and walked to Greta Hall where we had been boarders at Keswick School. We took the bus to Cockermouth and Grasmere and the launch round Derwentwater. The weather was lovely. This outing surpassed all our other holidays – happy memories!

WEDDINGS

MARRIED AT
ST. NICHOLAS' CHURCH,
PENTON.
SEPTEMBER 2ND, 1955.

JOAN STORY.

WITH
MR. & MRS. JAMES ROBSON'S
COMPLIMENTS.

VALLEY VIEW,
NEWCASTLETON,
ROXBURGHSHIRE.

Our wedding: 2nd September 1955. James McVittie Robson from Valley View, Newcastleton, father: Robert Temple Robson, a Road Worker. Margaret Joan Story, from Craigburn, Penton, father John James Story, deceased.

Jim, Joan and Davine

During the many years working for Lady Emma (Cavendish) Tennant, Jim and I were invited to three Tennant family weddings. To celebrate 50 years at Shaws Farm we were invited to Sunday lunch in a marquee at Roughly. It was a huge affair and so very enjoyable.

Joan Robson

Harland and Isabella (nee Reed)'s wedding October 1954 at Hayden Bridge near Hexham.

Jean and Jim Kirkpatrick's wedding – Last wedding at Castleton Old Church. My Jim is a guest on the right.

Joanna and John's Wedding, Australia 2006.

Joan Robson

Anne

Sandy and Anne's wedding, 2006

Jane and Andrew's wedding 2015

John Graham and Maria Armstrong's Wedding, Otterburn Towers 2001

At Eddie Tennant's wedding, his father, Toby read the Gaelic Grace. It was one of the loveliest things I had ever heard. I have never heard it since and it really was quite special.

A Gaelic Blessing
May the road rise to meet you,
May the wind be always at your back.
May the sun shine warm upon your face,
May the rain fall softly on your face
And may God hold you in the hollow of his hand.

"Don't Tell the Bride" – My grandson Jamie (Jane's boy) and Michelle's Wedding 2015

Inspired by the TV show *Don't Tell the Bride*, Michelle's employer, Cosatto, who make pushchairs, arranged a one-of-a-kind wedding for Michelle and Jamie. The theme was Alice in Wonderland and All things Wacky.

I will give you this story in Michelle's own words:

"Once a year, my boss offers employee's the chance to win up to £10,000 to do something they've always wanted to do – this is the Cosatto once in a lifetime award. People nominate themselves and tell everyone what they would do should they win. In 2015 I nominated myself and Jamie to get married with the money but with a twist. We wanted to do something memorable and unconventional. We planned to have team Cosatto to plan our wedding – 'Don't tell the bride,' style. This was the second time I had nominated us and with £10,000 at stake and up against an employee count of 50 people, we didn't think we had a chance.

A few weeks later we found out we were in fact down to the top three!

On the 16th April 2015, the results of the vote were in. we didn't get a wink of sleep the night before as it started to dawn on us we could really win this. On the day of the results we were in work only half the day that day as we were getting ready to travel to the borders for Jane's wedding. We thought we would miss the results which were due to be announced in the afternoon but out of the blue they changed the time. I sat there with the other competition nervously waiting for the outcome when our names were shouted out. - We had won!

The company created a Cosatto team of wedding planners and along with help from Jamie, planned every last detail of our Don't tell the Bride wedding. And they didn't tell the bride anything. All I was to know was the date and the time of the wedding. Every other detail was kept a secret.

On the 28th November 2015 I was collected from home with my dad, Ella and Jessica in a horse drawn Cinderella style carriage and made my way to the venue. The weather was definitely not for weather for an open Cinderella carriage.

We arrived at the beautiful Bolton school and walked down the aisle at 2 pm with my four bridesmaids. The ceremony was bright and colourful, just like Cosatto, with rainbows, balloons and glitter. I wore a white lace tea length dress with red sparkly shoes like Dorothy. Jamie looked handsome in his suit, bowler hat and fox tail!

The reception was like a complete fairy tale, decorated with more balloons and colour. Alice in Wonderland style. We had afternoon tea, candy floss, popcorn, flame throwers, knife jugglers, men on stilts and a huge pink flamingo wedding cake."

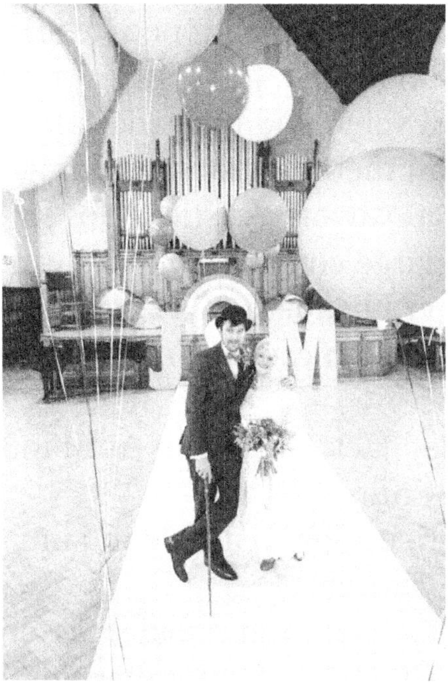
J M

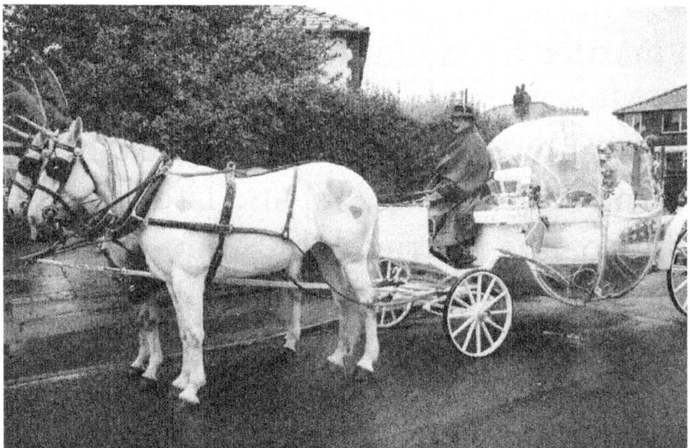

Jim and I attended many weddings over the years:

Harland married Isabella (nee Reed) in October 1954 at Haydon Bridge.

My cousin Evelyn and husband John Moore married 1956. They had their diamond wedding celebration in the Big Hall at Naworth castle. A lovely lunch was enjoyed by a large company of family and friends. Their daughter Elizabeth was married to Philip Howard of Naworth castle. Unfortunately she died in 2014.

Jane married Jack Lawson in April 1962 at Nicholforest Church.

Isabel married Alan Teasdale in January 1967 at Nicholforest Church.

Margaret married John (Jackie) Sisson at Nicholforest Church in September 1965.

Ann married Sandy Anderson at Kelso, Jane married Andrew Murray in the Grapes Hotel, Newcastleton. Anne's daughter Maria married John Graham at Otterburn Hall Hotel in 2001 and later emigrated to Teneriffe. Joanna married John Atkinson in Melbourne, Australia in 2006.

There was also: Sandy Hardy and Freda, Fiona Tucker from the Liddesdale. Maria Sisson and Peter Armstrong, John Sisson and Caroline Johnston, Nicola Teasdale and Paul Didsbury, Susan Teasdale and Andrew Swainson, Geoffrey Lawson and Louise. Linda Story and John Dickenson, Jimmy Story and Pauline.

Kathryn Teasdale and Kevin Grey, Elizabeth Moore and Philip Howard, to mention just a few.

BIRTHS –

Skye and Kyle Atkinson, the family of my granddaughter Joan.

Ella and Jess Cunningham, the family of my grandson Jamie.

Imogen and Jack and Isaac Armstrong. Family of my grandson John and his partner Amanda Irving.

(Jack, Imogen and Isaac)

(My granddaughter, Eleanor, was born on a plane flying over Greece! They were flying home from Australia and it made headline news at the time. Jane was covered by insurance for 7 months' pregnancy and the baby arrived just as the 7 months were up!) –

Eleanor is now 40 and working in finance in Dubai! Many years passed before she got British citizenship. It was a very trying process. No country wanted to help.

FUNERALS

Unfortunately there have been many family member funerals. Mam, Mum (Grandmother), Grandfather, Grandad Beaty, brother Harland and his wife Isabel, my sister Jane and John Story's daughter, aged only 14 years are some that come to mind.

When someone died, there were no phones or transport to easily get around and inform the community of the death so Bidding cards (also called funeral cards or mourning cards) were printed. These were small black edged envelopes and cards given out to family and friends then after the funeral was over, the card served as a memento of the person and their life.

My grandfather Robert Story who died in 1921 at the age of 61 and who is interred in Bewcastle Churchyard.

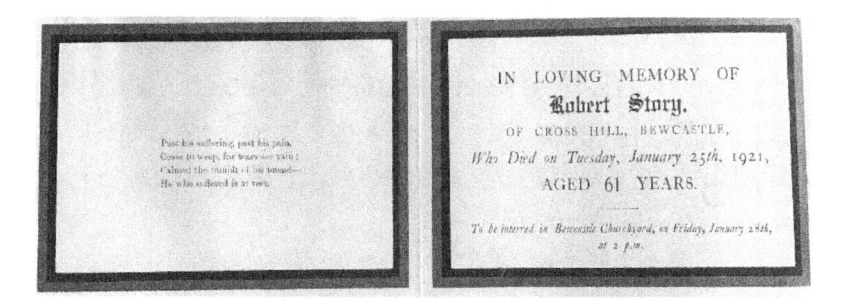

"Past his suffering, past his pain, Cease to weep, for tears are vain; Calmed the tumult of his breast – He who suffered is at rest."

My grandmother, Catherine (nee Ewart) Story who died in 1930 and is interred at Bewcastle Churchyard.

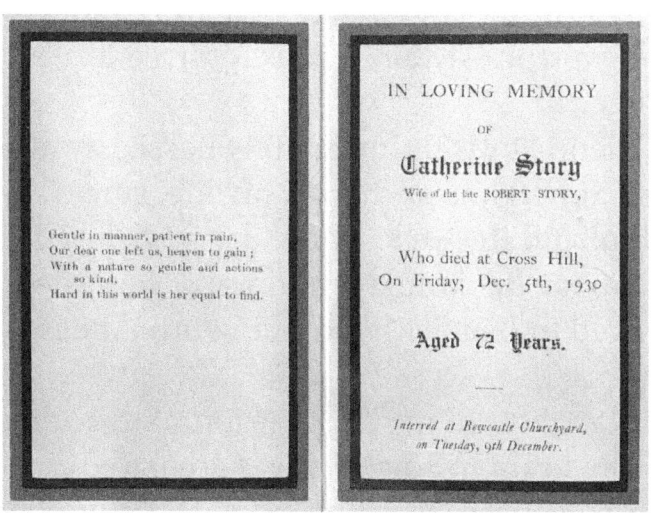

"Gentle in manner, patient in pain, Our dear one left us, heaven to gain; With a nature so gentle and actions so kind, Hard in this world is her equal to find."

My dad, John James Story died in 1934 at Bushley Bank and is interred at Bewcastle.

My mam, Kate (Catherine Little), died at Craigburn in 1963 and is interred at Bewcastle and my step-father Jim died in 1983 is interred at St. Cutherbert's Churchyard, Bewcastle.

In the year 1999 my sister Jane was diagnosed with cancer and sadly died on Christmas Eve. Jane was adored by everyone and her funeral at Nicholforest Church was huge.
My sister-in-law, Isabel Story (Harland's wife, nee Reed) passed away in 2001 and was interred in a cemetery at Haydon Bridge.
In 2003, my brother Harland passed away suddenly while building a stone dyke. He was interred at Haydon Bridge.
My good friend Doris unfortunately passed away a few years' ago. I had known her all my life, since primary school and Keswick school days. She used to go with me on our Big holidays and was a very special friend who lived in Bailey Mill in her youth. She is a sad loss.
Ria Story, daughter of my nephew John Story, died of cancer of the brain in 2015 and was cremated at Carlisle. A large congregation attended at a church in Haltwhistle. Ria played football for Haltwhistle under 15s girls in Northumberland. She was rushed to hospital after falling ill with a brain tumour and all her teammates posed for a photo to show her they were

missing her. Former Newcastle United and England hero Alan Shearer also joined in posing for a picture to show his support. Ria sadly died at the age of 14.

Jim's sister Jean was cremated at Edinburgh. His sister May was cremated at Carlisle and his mother and father were cremated at Carlisle.

Jim's niece Davine, her husband Trevor and their son Gordon are all interred at Darlington.

My niece Marie's husband is interred at Stapleton.

So many tributes too, to people in my life who have passed away. Too many, to share in this book but I would like to include some meaningful memories shared at my brother Harland, husband Jim and sisters Isabel and Jane's funerals as they were all such a big part of my life.

Joan Robson

Tribute to Harland Story (1928 – 2003)

It was a great honour and a bit of a relief to be asked to try and pay tribute to Harland today. A great honour because I am proud to have known Harland, and a relief because when Jimmy rang me I worried about what he was going to ask, as after Harland and I had attended a funeral a few years ago he asked me if when his time came I would mind slinging him on the front loader and driving him to Bewcastle. I am glad that idea was forgotten. But for Harland, I would have tried anything as I know Harland would have done anything that he possibly could for me or any other of his many friends.

It's hard to know where to start with Harland Story. Was any man more aptly named? Probably as with all good 'Stories' I should start at the beginning but I am well aware that it was only relatively late in his life that Harland and I got to know each other and although I sometimes feel I could easily find my way around Eskdalemuir or write a book on the 10 blowy days and the winter of '47 it was not until Harland was approaching retirement age that he moved into the cottage at Nilston Rigg. So I cannot begin to explain to you about his earlier life, of his great affection for Bewcastle, Newcastleton and Eskdalemuir and for his great love and loyalty to the Whitfield estate and his many friends there.

For the first few months I barely saw him as he was travelling in his old Lada car back to Whitfield to lamb at the Steel and was no doubt long gone before I was even out of bed. But gradually Harland became a regular part of life at Nilston Rigg and barely a day would go by without one of Harland's stories or his elaborate theories.

By the time Harland came to Nilston Rigg he was undoubtedly slowing down and he often remind me of an old collie dog, first into the passenger seat of the land rover, or perched on the back of the quad bike where he would wait patiently for someone to take him on a tour around the sheep or a trip out to some stone wall but the desire to work never left him. If he wasn't needed at Harsondale he would be in the pens at Nilston Rigg or the Lees with his favourite sparring partner my sister, Annabelle, counting sheep, not like most people by the head but by the number of legs or ears and generally trying to vex her.

Work was undoubtedly Harland's hobby and he believed it should be everyone else's hobby too as his reaction to finding Jimmy and Pauline daring to relax on a Sunday afternoon on SUN LOUNGERS in Harsondale's garden surely shows! For weeks after Harland muttered about setting fire to the offending sun loungers and we had to listen to a list of the alternative activities that Jimmy should have been carrying out, drains to mend, gates to hang and thistles to cut.

But there was much more to Harland's life than work. He took great interest in his family; his children Linda, Jimmy and John and his grandchildren. It gave him great pleasure to follow the progress of the famous Grand Bairns especially he took pleasure in seeing the development of Little Annabelle's (as she has to be known in Langley), interest in sheep. That the grandbairns share the same genes as Harland is indisputable. He recently told me that they claimed to have a dog that could catch moles by tapping on the hills and grabbing them when they put their heads out. What surprised me most was that Harland believed them. But he did tell me that HE had a dog that could sort fat lambs.

Harland's idea of leisure must surely have been moling; something which he had managed to turn into an art form, trapping, poisoning, gassing and no doubt his favourite of all FELLING. Anyone who showed the slightest interest in moling was an instant hit with Harland and an immediate recruit to the battle against the Mole, a battle which I fear Harland was never destined to win, and in which I had to suffer, often climbing into the tractor to go home at night to find that I had sat on the latest casualty.

Harland had the local Mole Road plan carefully mapped out and every journey we made together I would get updated figures on how each strategically placed trap was performing. When I pointed out a new molehill it was never from a Harsondale or Nilston Rigg mole but an invader from Robbie's or John Drydan and very occasionally Harland would have to admit to being baffled.

If Harland was not often baffled it is more than can be said of those around him; the triumph of Harland's day was to have baffled someone and it would be with great pride that he would report to me in the evening how his latest acquaintance didn't quite know what to make of him. One of his favourite tales was how after a rare fall out at Whitfield, Mr Blackett-Ord had told Harland exactly what he thought of him, to which Harland reported that he'd looked Mr Blackett-Ord in the eye and said, "Well Mr Blackett-Ord, now I know what YOU think about ME, but you don't know what I think about YOU." And walked off, no doubt leaving yet another baffled person in his wake.

And so to the end of the story, I was lucky enough to see Harland on the morning of his death, twice. Firstly to get the usual update on the Moling War and his latest strategy to get rid of some very persistent moles at Deanraw, and then later as he passed me with Ian, waving madly as he always did when we passed each other in vehicles. Harland was as keen and excited as he was on most days, looking forward, planning ahead and it is this that makes his sudden end such a great shock. But for me, it is exactly the way Harland would have wanted to go, not ailing in a hospital, not alone in the house, but sitting in Whitfield with a friend looking back onto Harsondale.

And for me, after that first sadness had passed, Harland's warmth and humour comes welling back up and as I look around me so many things remind me of him. Whenever I lift a bag of silage and see a worm, when I think about his weather predictions, Who wants to be a Millionaire, his unending optimism that he was about to win the Lottery, LUA, the relative merits of Wilf Mannion and Jackie Milburn, my continual battle to bag up barley for the cattle before he got it for the sheep, and of course, every molehill.

There are so many other attributes I can barely touch on, his devotion to his long-suffering wife Belle, the depth of which I never fully understood until her death. His great skills as a stockman, especially with sheep. His characteristic walk, spade over one shoulder, cap on, jacket buttoned up whatever the weather. Harland was truly unique.

There is an easy cliché often used at funerals but in this case it is truly appropriate: Harland Story, gone, but never forgotten.

Benedict Bates, 28th October 2003.

A tribute to: James McVitie Robson (1931 – 2020)

Jim Robson was a true Scot and a country man. He lived his life in the village, born in North Liddle Street and living at Valley View, once a hospital, buying his and Joan's first home in Langholm Street for the princely sum of £50, before living in Union Street where he and Joan spent 48 of the sixty four and a half years' they were married.

He worked in the forestry, then on the railways and was part of the protest on the night of the final train travelling through Newcastleton. Then Jim became Jimmy the Milk, but this role was so much more than just delivering milk. He also became his customers' handyman, helping out with any small repairs they might need doing, and his milk round could last a long time on some days. In the stormy winter of 1963, he took the children's sledge on the milk lorry and if he could not get the lorry to the customers, he would put crates of milk onto the sledge and trudge through the snow.

Then he had the sheep in the fields to look after and it was something Jim loved doing. His favourite Tup was more of a pet and Jim didn't only have it eating out of his hand but the tup literally took the food from his mouth! It was a sad time for him when he had to give that up.

He enjoyed a pint and would make sure that his trips were equally shared out amongst the bars in the village. He enjoyed the banter and would keep people entertained with his quick wit and stories from long ago. His favourite was remembering when there were only two cars in the village.

He was also a bit of a hoarder and it may take Joan some time to clear the sheds from all of the things he collected over the years. He would probably have had a great time looking through all the skips in the village recently and no doubt being given the okay to 'just take what you want Bizler,' filling the sheds with even more useful items that 'you never know when they might be needed.'

Jim was a well loved and liked character in the Liddesdale area; always happy to stop and have a chat. Unfortunately he because ill some years ago but stoically carried on even though his mobility became increasingly more difficult and it is not that long ago that we used to see him making his way round to Anne's on his walker, determined to make it on his own for as long as possible. He loved Joan and all his family deeply and will be greatly missed by all who knew him.

Isabel Catherine (Beaty) Teasdale
1944 – Dec 2022

Isabel was born in Bailey and when she was two years old moved to Craigburn Farm, Penton. She attended Warwicksland School and passed her 11 plus exam to go to Keswick School but she refused, not wanting to leave home. She left school at the age of 15 and her first job was in the offices of Braemar Woollen Mill, Hawick. She stayed with her big sister Joan in Newcastleton, travelling by train to Hawick every day. One of the perks of working for Braemar was being able to buy at discounted prices beautiful Cashmere jumpers. She worked for several years in hotels in Carlisle.

Isabel was invited to attend an interview at Oliver and Snowden's in Carlisle and after a general chat she was given some paper and asked to type a letter. She had never even seen a typewriter before let alone use one. She got the job! She could have wooed the manager with her extreme beauty and charm. Judith Brough also worked at Oliver and Snowden's and they immediately became great friends. They travelled to work together in Isabel's mini van, which strangely had the habit of running low on petrol. One solution was to put the foot on the accelerator to get home faster before they ran out! Another was to add water to the fuel tank hoping to dilute the petrol sufficiently to get home before running out completely. At some stage she stopped travelling and shared a flat or many flats in Carlisle with Margaret. They were also good at sharing their dresses and other clothes.

Isabel loved dancing and she and friend Annie walked to many local dances and always found a lift home. On a Saturday they would get the bus in Catlowdy to Carlisle, then another bus to the famous Heket and Cosmo dances. This is where Isabel met Alan. They fell in love immediately and one morning Jane came downstairs to find a note from Isabel: "Guess what – Alan has proposed and guess what, I have accepted." After not many months they married on 31st January and nine months later, honeymoon baby Nicola was born. Followed by Susan and Kathryn. They lived at Croft House Farm, Aughertree, later moving to Daleside Farm.

After some time, Isabel persuaded Alan to convert some of the beautiful courtyard out buildings into holiday cottages. They made a great success of a self-catering business with many guests becoming special friends, returning year after year. No wonder they did so well considering as a child, Isabel and sisters Jane and Margaret, had a good grounding. They would spend many an hour playing houses which they built with long tree branches on the ground. They would walk through the fields to the 'Tin Bit' at Hollywell Bridge where they would come home with all kinds of broken rubbish to furnish the fanciful house. Mam and Dad soon put an end to these adventures when they tried to bring home an old broken cooker which they had to abandon in the fields.

Isabel was very talented – she was a beautiful writer and needleworker making amazing tapestries, cross stitches and embroideries. She was encouraged by Alan's mam and in turn she taught her girls the same skills. She was a good baker, mouth-watering meringues, her speciality. She loved flower arranging, often decorating the Church for Christmas and other special occasions.

She and Alan were keen gardeners and for many years won the prestigious Cumbria Tourist Board Award for the best gardens and grounds. Isabel also enjoyed walking and the love of nature. Her first experience was when Joan arranged to meet her and they would hike to Skiddaw. There she was, all dressed in high heeled shoes and designer white jeans ready to go. She soon bought good walking boots and loved walking, often with the children, grand-children and collie dog.

There was nothing Isabel couldn't do, and do so well. Isabel – a truly loved, modest and very special person. She will be so sadly missed, loved and never forgotten.

Jane Forrester (Beaty) Lawson
(March 1942- December 1999)

Jane was one of the few people
Who was everyone's best friend.
Even when her life was in turmoil
She remained so to the end.
Her life was spent so loyally,
Her nature always giving.
She'll be missed so terribly
By those of us still living.
But let us take some comfort
From all that she was and had
And remember her with happiness
Although we feel so sad.
She was blessed with a happy marriage
To Jack and three fine lads
She was so very proud of them
And for that we should be glad.

Joan Robson

All of us are here today
Racked with pain and sorrow
But let us not forget
For Jane there is no pain tomorrow.
She fought her illness bravely
With courage and great faith,
More concerned for others
Than ever for herself.
We wonder! Why was she taken?
When others in this world are bad.
But God must have a special place for her
And that cannot be bad.
I don't suppose in all her life
Jane ever told a lie.
And on this very sad day
For this world is full of strife
Let us all be thankful
That we knew Jane through her life.
To know her was a privilege
Her heart was full of love.
God Bless you Jane and keep you
As you go to God above.

Joan's Journey – A Life well Lived

From the Family Album

Mum (Meg Newton)

Mam (Kate nee Little) and Harland

JOHN STORY (my father), Ina Moore, Mam (Kate nee Little), brother Harland. Mary Jane Moore (John Story's sister) with son Alan Moore on her knee and daughter Catherine Moore, arms folded.

Joan Robson

Mam and my sisters and me ready to ride to Sellafield – top left

Joan's Journey – A Life well Lived

Joan Robson

Sisters – Different flowers from the same garden

Jim and the floods in Newcastleton

Joan Robson

Maria and John

Jack, Imogen and Isaac

Skye and Kyle Atkinson
(Great grand son and Great grand daughter)

Above: Ella and Jess Cunningham

(Eleanor Cunningham, Jane Murray, Jamie and Fiona Cunningham)

Joan Robson

Brother in laws – Jack Lawson and Jackie Sisson – Always doing their bit for the community (around yr 2,000)

Kershopefoot Prisoner of War Camp

Newcastleton around 1916

Langholm Street, Newcastleton 1926

Bewcastle 2021

Joan Robson

Greenhaugh, home of Mum Newton. Then and now, taken from same angle.

OUR FAMILY TREE

Our family paternal lineage - From past research and research in February 2023 by Carole Somerville.

The Story Family

My Father: JOHN JAMES STORY was born on 14 May 1900 in Bewcastle when his father, ROBERT, was 41 and his mother, Catherine, was 41. He married my mother, CATHERINE (Kate) LITTLE in January 1931 in Longtown, Cumberland. They had two children during their marriage, my brother Harland and myself.

At 10 months old, in 1901, my father is listed in the census as living with his father, a shepherd and mother at Holme Head, Bewcastle and grandfather, JAMES EWART, a farmer (then a widow) and his Uncles Joseph, John and William Goodfellow and his aunts Kate and Grace.

John and Catherine's son, Harland was born in 1928 and their daughter Margaret JOAN, born 1934. John died of stomach Cancer on 18 February 1934, aged 33.

My grandfather, ROBERT (Dollan) STORY was born in 1859 in Bewcastle. He married CATHERINE (Kate) Ewart on 28 July 1888 in his home parish. The marriage register shows:

1888 Robert, shepherd, Pattenside, father, John, shepherd, married Catherine Ewart, Holmhead, father

James Ewart, Farmer. They had seven children in 17 years and he died on 25 January 1921 age 62.

Their family were:
1 Margaret b. 1889 who married Andrew Jeffrey and had Kitty, George and Desmond.
2 Mary Jane b. 1892 who married ... Beattie and had Oliver and (b), Andrew Moore and had a son Robert James. On a headstone in Bewcastle Church Yard is the following: "Andrew Douglas Moore died 8th July 1971 aged 80. Also his dear wife Mary Jane who died 25th April 1943 aged 51 and their son Robert James who died March 1930 aged 8 years.
3 Catherine b. 1894 who had Andrew b. 1920 at Hillhead. Kate married Jos. Bell and had Lewis who lived at Cummersdale.
4. Grace b. 1897 who married Robert Foster (Bobbie the Blacksmith). They lived at Lukes House and had Cathie and Thomas.
5. John James b. 1900, my father.
Dollan and Kate lived for some time at Holmhead and all their family were born there. At that time Dollan herded at the Beck and was an excellent sheep man. From Holmhead they moved to Gillerbeck and while there the family attended Bailey school. From Gillerbeck they moved to Deloraine in Yarrow and Jack, my father, attended Kirkhope School. Soon they moved to Bewcastle, firstly to Hillhead then to Crosshill.
Dolan died at Crosshill in 1921. Kate, Oliver and my father continued to farm there until Kate died in 1930.

Probate: STORY, Robert of Crosshill, Bewcastle, Cumberland, farmer died 25 January 1921. Administration Carlisle 2 March to Catherine Story widow. Effects £1061 10s.

Going back another generation and my **grandfather Robert's parents were JOHN STORY and JANE NIXON.** When JOHN was born in 1819, his father JOHN was 32 and his mother, MARTHA, was 30. JOHN's MOTHER, MARTHA OLIVER died when John was only six years old on 23 May 1825 in Bewcastle. Sadly four years later, his brother Thomas died in January 1829 at the age of 20. He lost his sister, Mary Story in 1840.

In 1841, JOHN, a mason apprentice was living at Coldslop in Nixons township, in Bewcastle with his father JOHN STORY, a stone mason, his brothers Robert and Thomas who were mason apprentices.

At that time there was a great deal of stonemason work in Bewcastle. Farms, houses and stonedykes were being erected and it is said that the Story family was greatly involved in much building work in the parish.

His father JOHN Story died in 1847 when JOHN was 28. Four years later, in 1851, JOHN married JANE NIXON on 25th June 1851 at Gretna Green. JOHN was still living in Coldslope, now listed in the census as a

Shepherd. He also had living with him a Boarder, Thomas Hogg, stonemason and journeyman.

They had nine children in 16 years:

John Story, born 1820, married Jane and their children were:
1. John b. 1852 at Coldslope. He married Mary Cowan at Bailey Head and had John b. 1877
2. Thomas b. 1855 who married Sarah Armstrong and had John James Armstrong b. 1886 died 1892 at Coldslope and Sarah Jane b. 1890.
3. Joseph b. 1856.
4. Robert b. 1859 (my grandfather)
5. Martha b. 1861, died 1861 at Cresshill.
6. William b. 1862 married Ellen Elliot of Flatt in 1887 and had: Mary b. 1888 at Highonset, John b. 1889 at Parkgate, Sybil Jane b. 1890 at Parkgate and Bessie b. 1896 at Lyneholmford.
7. Mary Jane b. 1865 died 1896.
8. James b. 1867 died 1867
9. James b. 1868 who married Margaret Beattie of Broadside and had John b. 1892 at Broadside died 1939 at Hillend, not married. Elisabeth Jane b. 1898 at Broadside, died 1975 at Damfoot Cottage. Little Jane as she was known never missed a day at school, a remarkable achievement as she had to walk from Broadside to Park School. For this she received a medal.

Listed as attending Bewcastle Church School in 1863 and 1864 were Joseph, son of John and Jane Story of Coldslope and Robert, son of John and Jane Story of Coldslope.

In 1861, at Coldslope, Nixons, JOHN STORY, shepherd was living with his wife JANE, and sons John, Thomas Joseph and ROBERT.

Still at Coldslope, Nixons in 1871, JOHN STORY, shepherd is living with his wife JANE, sons John, ROBERT, Joseph and William and daughter Mary Jane.

In 1881 at Coldslop Cottage, JOHN STORY, shepherd, was 62 and living with his 53-year-old wife JANE and sons Robert and William (shepherds) and James, a 13-year-old scholar.

JOHN STORY died at Broadside, Bewcastle in 1897 at the age of 78. His wife JANE died at Pattenside in 1889.

JOHN'S father, JOHN STORY was born in 1787/1788 in Bewcastle when his father THOMAS was 30 and his mother MARGRET was 22. He was baptised at Bewcastle on 28th January 1788.

JOHN married MARTHA OLIVER of Crosshill in Bewcastle on 1st July 1808. Both were under 21 years at the time of their marriage. They married with consent of their parents.

Their son Thomas was born in Bewcastle in 1809, their daughter Mary was born in 1811 and son James was born in 1814. James died in the same year when he was less than one year old. In 1816, their son James was born and in 1819, JOHN was born. Followed by son Robert in 1820. When JOHN was 38 years old, his wife MARTHA passed away on 23 May 1825 in Bewcastle at the age of 36. They had been married 16 years.

JOHN STORY died in 1847 at Coldslope in Bewcastle when he was 60 years old.

His father, THOMAS STORY was born in 1757 in Bewcastle. At the time his father THOMAS was 40 and his mother JANE was 36. He was baptised on 10th April 1757, "Son of Thomas Story of Mains."

He married MARGRET (nee STORY) on 23 October 1785 when he was 28 years old. "Thomas, a stonemason of the Row, Mains, Margret lived at Muckleyett.

Their daughter Jenny was born in 1786 in Bewcastle and their son JOHN in 1787.

THOMAS STORY died on 29 November 1830 in Bewcastle when he was 73 years old.

His father THOMAS STORY was born on 20 August 1717 in Bewcastle and Baptised on 20 August 1717, son of LEONARD STORY in Bewcastle. His father LEONARD died at Kinkryhill, Bellbank, Bewcastle when THOMAS was five years old.

THOMAS married JANE TAYLOR on 2nd May 1750 in Bewcastle and they had eight children: Mary (1751), William (1752), George (1754), John (1755), Margaret (1755), THOMAS (1757), Patrick (1759) and Jane (1761).

THOMAS died at the age of 76 in 1793 at Bewcastle.

(Information about Mains from the Bewcastle Parish Registers: Two farms of the same name, the farmhouses adjacent to each other. In the 18th century they amalgamated into a farm of 50 acres, but in the late 19th or early 20th century it was absorbed into Row and Flatt farms. Grass covered foundations remain).

His father LEONARD STORY was born in 1672, the son of JOHN STORY and MARGRET LITTLE. LEONARD was aged 40 when he got married.

LEONARD married ANN ROUTLEDGE on 12 June 1712 in Bewcastle. They had five children in ten years. Adam (1713), Mary (1713 Kinkyryhill, Belbank, Bewcastle), Arthur (1717, Kinkryhill, Belbank, Bewcastle (THOMAS (1717).

His son John passed away in 1721 at the age of 14. LEONARD STORY died on 30th October 1722 in Kinkryhill, Belbank, Bewcastle, when he was 50 years old and is buried in St. Cuthbert's Churchyard, Bewcastle.

(Against north churchyard wall): Here lies Leonard Story of Bewcastle, who died on October the 30 A.D. 1722, aged 50 years. And his son John, who died June the 29 1721, aged 14. And his son Adam, who died Sept. the 3 1731, aged 17 years. And his son Arthur, who died August the 29 1757 aged 40 years. Also here lies the body of Eleanor, wife to Adam, who died August 13 1771 aged 42 years.

Joan's Journey – A Life well Lived

Story Family and Ewarts

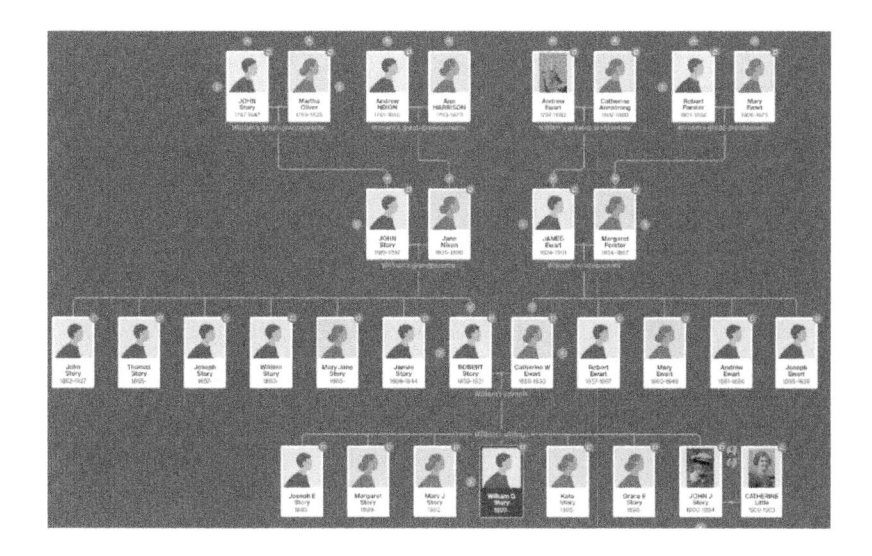

EWART LINEAGE

My father, JOHN JAMES STORY's mother was CATHERINE WILLIAM ARMSTRONG EWART BORN ON 10TH April 1858 at Bewcastle. When she was born, her father, JAMES was 23 and her mother, MARGARET FORSTER was 23. She married ROBERT STORY on 28 July 1888 in Bewcastle (as detailed above).

CATHERINE was born on 10 April 1858 in Bewcastle. She died at the age of 72 in 1930 at Cross Hill, Bewcastle.

Probate: Catherine William Armstrong of Cross Hill Bewcastle Cumberland widow died 5 December 1930. Administration (with Will) Carlisle 19 January to John James Story farmer. Effects £283 19s. 8d.

Her father JAMES EWART was born on 23 June 1834 at Holmhead, Bewcastle. When he was born his father ANDREW was 37 and his mother CATHERINE (nee ARMSTRONG) was 27. He married MARGARET FOSTER on 17 August 1856. They had five children during their marriage: Robert (1857-1867), CATHERINE WILLIAM ARMSTRONG EWART (1858-1930), Mary (1860-1946), Andrew (1861-1886) and Joseph (1865-1939). JAMES died in 1901 at Holmhead, Bewcastle at the age of 66.

His father ANDREW EWART was born in May 1797 at Beyond the Moss, Nicholforest. When ANDREW was born, his father, JOHN EWART was 25 and his mother ELIZABETH ROUTLEDGE was 38. He married CATHERINE ARMSTRONG on 25 November 1826 in Bewcastle. They had 12 children in 32 years and he died in April 1882 in Longtown after having lived a long life of 84 years.

Children to ANDREW EWART and CATHERINE ARMSTRONG: William (1827-1903), John (1829-1868), Andrew (1833-1906), JAMES (1834-1901), Mary Armstrong Ewart (1836-1910), Andrew (1838-1892), Elizabeth (1840-1881), Janet Armstrong (1842-1959), Grace (1844-1900), Catherine (1847-1925) and Alexander (1859).

FORSTERS:

My great grandmother on my father's side, was MARGARET FORSTER.

MARGARET FORSTER was born on 15 December 1834 to ROBERT and MARY. MARGARET married JAMES EWART on 17 August 1856 in Bewcastle and they had five children: Robert *1857), CATHERINE WILLIAM ARMSTRONG (1858), Mary (1860), Andrew (1861) and Joseph (1965). Margaret died at the age of 32 at Longtown on 15 July 1867.

Her father ROBERT FORSTER was born on 24 September 1801 at Netheroakshaw, Belbank, Bewcastle. When he was born his father ARTHUR was 42 and his mother, ELIZABETH WRIGHT was 34. He married MARY EWART on 15 July 1826 in Bewcastle. They had 11 children in 21 years. ROBERT died on 28 August 1856 in Bewcastle at the age of 54.

Their children: Robert Ewart (1826 Bewcastle), Elizabeth (1828 Bewcastle), Nanny (Annie, Castleton, Roxburghshire) (1830), Mary (1833, Castleton), Margaret (1834, Castleton), Arthur (1836, Castleton), Jane (1839, Bewcastle), Henry (1843-1846), Joseph (1843-1890, Longtown District birth), Sybil (1845 at Crook Burn, Bailey, Bewcastle) and Thomas (1847, Bewcastle).

ROBERT'S father, ARTHUR FORSTER was born about 1759 at Nicholforest and died in 1851.

THE LITTLES

My Mother, CATHERINE (Kate) LITTLE was born in 1909 in Bellingham, Northumberland. Her father WALTER DODD LITTLE, was 41 when she was born and her mother MARGARET JANE YOUNGER NEWTON was 36. CATHERINE married JOHN JAMES STORY when she was 22 years old and they had two children together, myself and my brother Harland. She also had three daughters with James Forrester Beaty. My mother died on 18 July 1963 at the age of 54.

In 1911, two-year-old Kate lived at Kirnsyke, Gilsland with her father, WALTER DODD LITTLE, then 42, a shepherd, her mother MARGARET JANE LITTLE and her sisters: Bella Mary, Annie Jane, Florence Sarah, Margaret Newton Little and 1 month old Jessie Little and her 9-year-old brother Walter Dodd Little.

Her father WALTER DODD LITTLE was born on 11 April 1868 at the Green in the Parish of Shitlington High, Wark in Bellingham. His father, WILLIAM was 52 and his mother, Jane was 33 when he was born.

WALTER DODD married MARGARET JANE YOUNGER NEWTON in January 1895 in Bellingham. They had eight children in 15 years. He died in 1941 in Border, Cumberland at the age of 73 and was buried in Falstone Northumberland.

Their children: Edward William (1896), Bella Mary (1898), Annie Jane (1900), Walter Dodd (1902), Florence Sarah (1904), Margret Newton (1908), CATHERINE LITTLE (1909-1963) and Jessie (1911)

WALTER's father WILLIAM LITTLE was born on 25 January 1816 in Bewcastle. He married JANE DODD on 11 September 1858 in Wark, Northumberland. They had five children in 16 years. He died on 15 February 1908 in Northumberland at the impressive age of 92 at Paddaburn, Northumberland. Their children: William (1859-1897, The Green, Shitlington High, Northumberland), Sarah (1864-1941, the Green, Shitlington High, Northumberland), WALTER DODD LITTLE (1868-1941, the Green, Shitlington High, Northumberland), John (1875-1947, Wark, Northumberland).

The DODDS and the ARMSTRONGS

Moving on to JANE DODD who married WILLIAM LITTLE and this takes us further back to our Dodd and Armstrong ancestors from Paddaburn, Greystead in Northumberland. The fells in this area with their ruined castles, old bastles (defensible farmsteads) and pele towers are indication of its turbulent past. The defensible houses grew out of the need to protect the community from the lawless Reivers that roamed the border areas. The ARMSTRONGS, DODDS and ROBSONS are among Reiver surnames.

Paddaburn

JANE DODD was born on 18th March 1835 at Kershopehead, Bailey, Bewcastle. When she was born, Her father WILLIAM was 25 and her mother, ISABELLA was 23. She married WILLIAM LITTLE in 1858 in Wark. They had five children in 16 years and she died on 16 June 1917 having lived a long life of 82 years. Jane was buried in Falstone, Northumberland.

JANE'S father, WILLIAM DODD was born on 16 April 1809 in Greystead and was baptised on 27 April 1809 (Presbyterian, Falstone, Northumberland). He married ISABELLA ARMSTRONG on 18th November 1834 in Gretna Green, Dumfrieshire, Scotland. The couple had 11 children in 19 years and he died on 29th December 1893 at the age of 84. WILLIAM was buried in Newcastleton.

When WILLIAM and ISABELLA got married, he told the official that he was a tinker as he feared to be charged at a higher rate if he was known to be a farmer! (source: *"Runic inscription on Hazel-Gill Crags, near Bewcastle" by W L Charlton, Archaeologica aeliana, Vol 17, 1895).* On Page 53 the writer describes when he had occasion to ride over the fells to Bewcastle. A road that is merely a track, hardly distinguishable from a sheep track. They accepted the hospitality of Mr. Dodd, tenant of Paddaburn (a farm which was formerly part of the Hesleyside estate, on the banks of the Irthing). Mr Charlton described Mr. Dodd as being advanced in years and he acted as their guide the next morning riding with them to Bewcastle. Mr Dodd entertained them with many tales of past days and people, on their journey including an account of his own wedding at Gretna Green, many years previous. He had given them worthy who officiated on that occasion 'to understand that he was but a tinker, lest he should be charged a fee on a higher scale as a farmer.'

Gretna Marriage Records 1834

"Nov 20 1834 – William Dodd from the parish of Greystead within County of Northumberland, and Isabella Armstrong from the parish of Bewcastle, Cumberland was married before these witnesses John Sowerby and Sarah Sowerby ..."

Another tale about William that has been passed down through the family is that William Dodd (1809) born in Liddesdale, married Isabella Armstrong (1811) over the Kershope Burn Border in 1834. The Minister realised that he could not legally marry them at the Bride's home in Kershopehead in England, so they crossed the burn into Scotland where the marriage was legal. The marriage was registered at Gretna. They then moved to Northumberland where he continued to work as a shepherd. He is recorded as being a farmer in 1871 and in 1881 he farmed 850 acres. 10 years later, he farmed 3400 acres.

WILLIAM and ISABELLA's children: JANE (1835 Kershopehead, Bailey, Bewcastle). Helen, Mary, Walter, Margaret William, John Senhouse, James, Catherine, Adam and Robert.

In 1851 according to the census, the family is living at Smalesmouth and William is a shepherd (definitely in the genes!). In 1861 the family are living at Chindyke, Smalesmouth William, now listed as a farmer, and Isabella with their children Mary, Margaret, Johnes, Catherine, Adamand grandson Robert, son in law Wdilliam Little (shepherd) and a boarder Thomas Scott who is a gamekeeper.

In the farm adjacent, at Hopehouse, Smalesmouth, is WILLIAM'S father, WALTER DODD (farmer of 4000 acres, employing 2 men) and mother MARY, with their grown-up family, Walter (29 a shepherd), Margaret, Mary, Matthew, William, John and servants.

At the age of 71, WILLIAM DODD was at Smalesmouth, Greystead, a farmer of 3400 acres living with his family.

WILLIAM did on 29 December 1893 in Paddaburn Farm, Greystead and he was buried in Newcastleton.

PROBATE: DODD, William of Paddaburn, Greystead, Northumberland farmer died 29 December 1893. Probate Newcatle upon Tyne 14 February to John Senhouse Dodd, farmer. Effects £478 7s. 6d.

Joan Robson

TRANSCRIPT OF DODD FAMILY MEMORIAL AT CASTELTON CEMETARY, SCOTTISH BORDERS:

In memory of
William Dodd who died at Paddaburn on 29th December 1893 aged 84 years. Isabella Dodd his wife who died at Paddaburn on 31st June 1891 aged 78 years. Walter their son who died at Churn Syke 27th August 1858 aged 29 years. Mary Dodd their daughter who died at Paddaburn on 31st January 1892 aged 55 years. William Dodd their son who died at Brampton on April 111th 1932 aged 88 years.

WILLIAM'S father is: WALTER DODD and his mother: MARY ARMSTRONG. WALTER DODD was born around 1770 in Paddaburn.

WALTER married JANE and according to his gravestone at Old Castleton Cemetery, their children were: William, Jane (1911-1813), Jane (1813-1813), Jane (1817-1818), James, Margaret and John.

A Life Well Lived ...

Life is a journey and not always a smooth one. All we can do is navigate the twists and turns, push through the challenges and try to live to our fullest potential. I grew up in a remote farming community during the disruption and hardship of war when food and other commodities were rationed and people showed strength and unity in the face of adversity. I have travelled the world and learned about different cultures, places and people. I have worked hard and gained many skills. I have known love and happiness and joy but also sadness, pain and loss. My life hasn't been easy ... but it has been a life well lived.

In Conclusion ...

No more:

Adventures and Outdoor Activities
Committee Memberships, Creating and Cleaning
Driving
Fund Raising
Gardening and Farming, Sheep and Cattle
Hay making, Hens and Holidays
Marmalade and Jam Making
Rug making and Crook Making
Walking and volunteering ...

But a lifetime worth of memories to look back upon, to cherish and to share.

"May love and laughter light your days and warm your heart and home.
May good and faithful friends be yours, wherever you may roam.
May peace and plenty bless your world with joy that long endures.
May all life's passing seasons bring the best to you and yours!"

(Irish Blessing)

Printed in Great Britain
by Amazon